AGENCY ADDA

THE ULTIMATE AGENCY BLUEPRINT

ARCHANA PUROHIT

INDIA • SINGAPORE • MALAYSIA

ISBN
Paperback 979-8-89632-362-4
Hardcase 979-8-89699-506-7

CONTENTS

To my artistic mother- Anjali Purohit,
who taught me that creativity has no bounds,
dreams no deadlines and learning has no expiry date…

ACKNOWLEDGMENTS

What a ride! And what a journey this has been — from the wild world of brainstorming to the final page-turner you now hold in your hands. Writing *Agency Adda* wasn't just about penning a book; it was about surviving the madness, juggling deadlines, battling inner critics, and perhaps slightly over-caffeinating. But like any good story, it had its fair share of heroes, and here's where I take a moment to say *thank you* to the incredible people who made this possible.

To my first reader, Upasana, you were my sounding board, and yes, the person who was pulled into a litter of half-baked drafts. I could count on you to wade through my mess of ideas and remind me of my own brilliance (on good days), and the need for a strong edit (on bad days). You made sure this book went from chaos to clarity.

To my first teacher and the ultimate stress manager, my mom, you've always been my go-to for advice — both life and word-related. And of course, for helping me manage the occasional endorphin boost via chocolate or a motivational talk. I couldn't have asked for a better emotional support coach.

My grandfather, Shri Banwarilal Ji Purohit, for being my North star and whose life is an inspiration, for me and thousands of others. I will always strive towards being a better person each day, with your unconditional blessings and love.

To Ankur, my husband, for putting up with my PMS *and* PWS (Pre-Writing Syndrome, yes, it's a thing!). You patiently listened to my rants, validated my crises, and offered support with the frequency of an enthusiastic cheerleader — all while pretending you didn't notice my ever-growing pile of coffee cups, and rieling printer in our home office.

To my son, Divit, the original cheerleader, who kept telling me, "Mom, you got this!" — even when I wasn't sure myself. Your confidence in me means the world.

Papa, you're my rock. In the constant sea of doubt, thanks for grounding me with your wisdom and love. Especially on those days I thought the world was going to eat me alive.

A heartfelt thanks to my in-laws for tolerating my absence from countless dinners, family functions, and spontaneous get-togethers. You're the silent supporters who keep the ship sailing smoothly behind the scenes.

Friends, thank you for sticking by me during my frequent disappearances. The text messages, the kind words, and the occasional "Where are you?" — I promise, I was working... (sort of).

A special mention to my dietitian for putting up with my stress-eating and *actually* eating well while writing. And allowing me to pause the diet for the 10th time (I will not tell your other clients about this special treatment). I'm sure the book might have come out faster without all those chocolate breaks — but then, we both know where that would've ended!

To the founders in my first batch of coaching — yes, you were my guinea pigs, and I can proudly say, you survived (Testament that my ways work beyond me)! While you give me credit for helping you scale your business, well honestly you helped me grow as a Coach, and I'm grateful for that.

Jaya, my rockstar editor, thank you for keeping up with me as I rewrote and re-drafted, and let's not forget those endless typos I kept throwing your way. You've been patient beyond measure and somehow, you always made me look like I had my act together (which, let's be honest, was only an illusion you crafted).

A huge thank you to the incredibly talented illustrator, Lavanya, whose artistic brilliance brought my thoughts and boards to life. You've helped transform my words into visuals that truly make this book a pleasure to hold, look at, and read.

And thanks to you, my readers — thank you for holding this book in your hands. Your belief in me as a writer is what makes this all worth it. I'm so excited to share this journey with you, and I can't wait for you to dive into the pages of *Agency Adda*. Your feedback and support mean everything to me.

Last but not the least,an ode to the universe, and of course, to Shah Rukh Khan, who taught me that "Kisi cheez ko shiddat se chaaho toh puri kaynat use pane mein saath deti hai." ("If you desire something with all your heart, the entire universe conspires to help you achieve it."). Well this was before 'Manifestation' became the IT word.

I guess, it turns out, the universe did conspire after all. Let's keep chasing those dreams; Let's keep drafting those goals; Let keep our hopes & horses high; Because together we can.

With all my love,

Archana Purohit

FOREWORD

Agency Adda isn't your typical business book. It's a vibrant, practical guide designed to help you navigate the unpredictable world of running a service-based business. Whether you're just starting out or looking to scale, this book is packed with real-world insights, actionable strategies, and a generous dose of humour that makes even the most complex topics easy to digest. But before diving into the book, let me share a bit about how I first met Archana.

It was over 15 years ago when Archana, in her early twenties, walked into my office for an interview at Franchise India. She had come to meet our Editor for a role, but due to some change in schedule she met me. At that time, I was really impressed with her urge to grow and make a difference. I felt she was not a conventional professional applicant and had an entrepreneurial attitude. At Franchise India we like that and I recommended her to our editor and she did select her. Despite her young age, she was willing to take challenge and not very rigid on a KRA. She was hired our youngest Assistant Editor, but Archana wasn't just a journalist; she was a sharp, strategic who had an intuitive grasp of the inner workings of businesses. This unique perspective was one of the things that made her stand out.

Fast forward to today, and Archana has evolved into a remarkable entrepreneur in her own right. She's built and scaled her own agency, held CXO roles in others, and successfully guided businesses to profitability and sustainability. What sets her apart is her genuine commitment to adding value—not just to her own businesses, but to the entrepreneurial community as a whole.

Now, with *Agency Adda*, Archana brings all her hard-won knowledge and experience into one comprehensive guide for those looking to build profitable, scalable service businesses. This book is especially timely, as India continues to see a booming startup ecosystem. As the country's economy continues to evolve, there is a huge demand for agile service providers who can meet the needs of this fast-paced, ever-changing market.

What she focuses on in *Agency Adda* is something too often overlooked in the world of service businesses: profitability. Many entrepreneurs obsess over turnover, but what really matters is building a business that's not only sustainable but consistently profitable. This book emphasizes that growth is not just about increasing revenue—it's about streamlining operations, managing expenses, and building a solid foundation for long-term success.

India's startup ecosystem is vibrant, with new opportunities emerging almost daily. But with that growth comes complexity. Agencies, consultancies, and other service-based businesses must become agile, anticipating market shifts and positioning themselves as problem-solvers for clients. This book shows you how to do just that, whether it's carving out a niche, improving client relationships, or building a team that's capable of scaling with you.

Additionally, *Agency Adda* doesn't shy away from discussing the emotional side of entrepreneurship. Archana has always been open about the personal challenges of running a business—the pressure, the stress, and the constant need to adapt. But what's remarkable is how she's learned to manage those challenges with grace and focus, and that wisdom is reflected throughout the book. She doesn't just teach you how to scale your business; she teaches you how to stay grounded and keep your sanity intact along the way.

Agency Adda is more than just a business guide. It's a blueprint for navigating the world of service businesses with profitability, sustainability, and a healthy balance between work and life. If you're looking to transform your services business or start one or simply curious about what it takes to build a thriving business in today's dynamic ecosystem, this book is the resource you've been waiting for.

I've watched Archana grow from a young, ambitious journalist to an entrepreneur who has contributed greatly to the business world. Her journey has been nothing short of inspiring, and I'm excited for you to experience the wisdom she's distilled into *Agency Adda*. Trust me, you're in excellent hands.

Warm regards,

Sachin Marya

TAKING THE FIRST LEAP

There's a unique kind of person who looks at uncertainty and sees an opportunity. If you're holding this book, chances are you're one of them. You're right at the start of something new, where the thrill of what's possible meets the uncertainty of the unknown. It feels like that quiet moment right before a journey begins, one where the road ahead could lead to places you've only imagined. There's no rush, no race to win—just the path in front of you, waiting to unfold.

For me, this was the start of building a digital marketing agency—an adventure filled with both excitement and doubt. I remember standing there, unsure of where that first step would take me, but knowing it was the beginning of something real. Whether you're fresh out of college, a freelancer looking to expand, or someone ready to build something of your own, this journey has room for all of us. It's about discovery, growth, and creating something that could change your life and the lives of those you work with.

And here you are, ready to begin.

As you take that first leap, questions inevitably creep in: Where do I start, and how do I keep moving forward? These are the questions that keep so many aspiring entrepreneurs up at night and believe me, I've been there. When I set out to build my digital marketing agency, I faced the same uncertainties and lingering doubts.

But what I quickly realized was that starting this kind of business wasn't just about launching a venture—it was about stepping into the world of service. And service, in its truest sense, means putting the client at the center of everything. It's about serving their needs, solving their problems, and making their success your mission. With that focus comes immense responsibility, much like a bridge requires a solid foundation to bear the weight of everything that crosses it. Without a healthy structure in place to address this, entrepreneurs can find themselves merely self-employed, trapped in a repetitive cycle that lacks progression—like a hamster on a wheel, moving constantly but going nowhere.

Taking the first leap

This leads to service businesses being seen as less exciting, but the reality is that they hold immense potential for growth and evolution over time. When you build the right foundations by establishing solid processes, nurturing strong relationships, and focusing on adaptability, your agency becomes more than just a service provider. It becomes a resilient, adaptable, and innovative force, capable of weathering challenges and standing out in a crowded market. The key lies in doing it all with the right spirit, keeping service at the heart of everything you do.

And that's what Agency Adda is here for—to guide you in building that foundation, enabling you to thrive in this dynamic world rather than just get by.

This guide is born from my own journey, and trust me, when I was starting out, I would have given anything to have a resource like this at my side. I began my career as a journalist, constantly exploring creative outlets, but eventually, the idea of starting my own digital marketing agency took hold. I had a few lakhs to my name, a head full of ideas, and a heart full of determination. But within just a few months, the reality hit me hard—I found myself wondering if I'd even be able to make payroll.

I remember that every single day, I carried three gold *guineas* in my purse. It was a kind of insurance in my mind—a small safety net in case I couldn't land a client. If worse came to worst, I thought, at least I'd have something to trade. That's how uncertain things felt back then. What I really needed at that time was a mentor—someone who could guide me through the challenges without pouring negativity into the mix. But what I mostly received were warnings about how hard business is and how difficult it would be to succeed.

And yes, it *was* hard, but here's the thing: it was hard work, and more importantly, it was having a clear plan that made all the difference. I had to learn through trial and error that without structure, everything just falls apart. There had to be a method to the madness. Once I built that structure and put systems in place, I saw the change almost immediately. Within three weeks, I had landed three clients, and from that point on, I never had to worry about those gold *guineas* again.

Looking back, I realize that it wasn't luck or chance that got me through—it was the discipline to create a solid foundation for my agency. That's why this guide exists: to give you the knowledge and support I wish I had back then, so you don't have to face those moments of doubt alone.

Now, drawing from all the lessons I've shared in this guide, I can look back and say that I've built not one, but three successful agencies—each one born from the insights and hard-earned experiences I've gathered along the way. One of those agencies was even acquired, which is a journey in itself. From managing a 50 crore business to building systems that keep everything running smoothly, these are the insights I've gathered from my journey. But the key takeaway here is this: for every entrepreneur out there, success isn't about luck or some kind of mystical chance. It's about structure, strategy, and a willingness to do the hard work. When you have the right foundation, nothing is out of reach.

Today, while those agencies are humming along on the systems I've built for them, I've shifted my focus to staying relevant and creating even more impact. Over the past 12 months, I've ventured into business coaching, working with over 25 startup agencies. And the results? Incredible growth—some of these agencies have tripled their scale in just 180 days. These aren't just flukes or one-off success stories. Each win has validated the very strategies and frameworks I've laid out in this guide. I've seen firsthand how powerful they can be when put into action.

Now, it's your turn. With *Agency Adda*, you're standing at the edge of something big. This is your chance to take that first leap toward building and growing your own agency, rooted in stability and driven by a clear plan. And trust me, with the right structure, there's no limit to where you can go.

CHAPTER 1

YOUR AGENCY'S ORIGIN STORY

Imagine sitting down for coffee, flipping through those captivating rags-to-riches stories. The dream, right? To be the next big thing, shaking up the world. We've all been there, haven't we? Mapping out our path to be the next Bill Gates or Steve Jobs, fueled by ambition and inspiring tales. But sometimes, we get lost in these dreams without pausing to understand where we truly belong in the grand scheme of things. It's easy to get caught up in the hustle narrative or compare ourselves to those who seem to have made it, forgetting about our own unique advantages or challenges along the way.

But success isn't a one-size-fits-all thing. The tech genius who revolutionises software isn't on the same path as someone whose genius is in literature. It's important to understand your own archetype, your unique blend of skills, passions, and quirks that set you apart. You gotta craft your own strategy, recognise where you need support, and build bridges to cross future challenges. It's like having a heart-to-heart with yourself about who you are, what makes you passionate, and the hurdles you'll overcome. This deep dive into your identity is the first step in creating the blueprint for your future digital marketing agency. It shapes your path and the soul of your agency - its vibe and its essence.

As we journey through the diverse world of digital agency founders, let's unpack the different archetypes. It's an opportunity for you to discover what resonates with you. Are you a mix of different qualities? Or do you stand out in your own unique way? This exploration is crucial in finding your niche and creating an agency that truly reflects who you are.

THE FREELANCING FIREFLY

Let's start with a group I like to call the Freelancing Fireflies. These are the folks who have carved out their own space in the digital world, not just exploring it, but owning it. They're the tech experts who can squash bugs with ease, the designers whose work you've admired on social media, or the marketing pros who can make a hashtag trend overnight. Well, if you're nodding along, thinking, "Hey, that sounds like me," you're probably one of them. It's time to shine a light on those strengths you've been polishing over the years. You've got the insights, the flexibility, and a toolkit that's the envy of many. But, as they say, with great power comes great responsibility.

Shifting from flying solo to leading your own agency brings its own set of challenges. You'll be managing a team, tackling the finance game, and learning to grow beyond what you already know. Sure, it can feel daunting, but that's where the magic happens—right when you step into the unknown. And trust me, you've got what it takes to make it happen.

For all you Freelancing Fireflies, here's something to ponder: your path is unique, filled with standout achievements and moments you'd prefer to forget. Each challenge you face is an opportunity for growth, a chance to gain new skills, and a way to prepare for the successes ahead.

THE LIFESTYLE HUSTLERS

In the bazaar of the digital age, you might just be what I like to call a Lifestyle Hustler. You're one of those sharp entrepreneurs who knows how to turn every opportunity into a thriving digital venture. You may not be the one crafting the content or designing the graphics, but your genius lies in spotting potential and turning it into something real, something impactful.

Wondering if this is you? Here's a quick test: Are you constantly connecting dots, making deals, and seeing business opportunities where others see nothing but roadblocks? If so, you might be a Lifestyle Hustler in the making.

Your superpower lies in your business acumen, your ability to predict the next big thing, and your talent for rallying the right people around your vision. It's about understanding the market pulse, just like digital dynamos Social Beat or Schbang, who didn't just ride the wave but created ripples of their own in the Indian market with their forward-thinking approaches.

Yet, every entrepreneur faces hurdles, and Lifestyle Hustlers are no exception. The challenge often lies in self-promotion and personal branding. It's essential to emerge from the shadows and claim your spot in the limelight, showcasing your journey and achievements as a badge of honour. When growth plateaus, that's not your cue to take a break but a sign to shake things up. Whether it's diversifying your services, tapping into new markets, or embracing the latest tech trends, there's always room for growth and innovation.

Keeping pace with the digital world's rapid evolution requires consistently leveling up your skills and strategies. It's about finding that creative yin to your entrepreneurial yang—someone who shares your vision and helps you reach new heights, allowing you to focus on broader horizons.

For those who see themselves as Lifestyle Hustlers, know this: your journey is defined by the bold moves you make, the partnerships you cultivate, and the innovative paths you forge. Embrace the challenges as opportunities to grow, lean into your strengths, and continuously seek ways to innovate.

THE MNC MONGERS

If you're one of the seasoned pros who's traded the corporate trenches for the digital marketing playground, you're part of a unique breed shaking up the industry—the MNC Mongers. You know the ins and outs of nailing boardroom presentations and tackling office dynamics. Now, it's time to bring that wealth of experience to a new frontier.You're the type who can strategise a digital campaign with the same finesse you used to navigate corporate strategy. Your superpower lies in bringing a dash of corporate sophistication to the digital Wild West.

Now, you're bringing that wealth of experience to the digital marketing playground.

You're the type who can strategize a digital campaign with the same finesse you used to tackle corporate strategies. Your superpower? It's blending corporate sophistication with the fast-paced energy of the digital landscape. You've got a suitcase full of skills just waiting to be unpacked—think operational efficiency, project management, expertise with CRM tools, and an eye for strategic planning. You're the bridge that connects the methodical approach of the corporate world with the creative, dynamic flair of digital marketing.

But let's be honest, it's not always a smooth transition.The startup hustle is a whole new beast to tame. Trading in your shiny corporate shoes for sneakers might mean learning to move at a faster, more unpredictable pace. And then there's the challenge of stepping out from behind the corporate logo. Personal branding becomes key, and it's time to shine under your own banner and let the world see what you're capable of.

Let me tell you about a friend, Karan, who's a true MNC Monger. After a decade in telecom, he leapt into digital marketing with nothing but a vision and his corporate playbook. The biggest shock? The pace! The startup world was a sprint, not the marathon he was used to. But by playing to his strengths and learning on the fly, Karan's now running a digital agency that's the talk of the town, appreciated for his methodological approach and corporate finesse.

For those MNC Mongers ready to take the plunge, remember: your corporate armor is invaluable, but don't be afraid to swap it for a digital cape when needed. Find your groove, partner with creative geniuses who complement your structured approach, and dive into the hustle with an open mind. And don't forget—your network and connections will always carry forward, opening doors and opportunities as you transition into this new space.

THE ACCIDENTAL HERO

Have you ever wandered through the digital maze, not really looking for anything specific, and then, out of nowhere, you struck gold? If so, welcome to the club of what I call "Fatepreneurs," or Accidental Heroes. It seems like the universe might have had a grand plan for you to dive into the agency game—a twist in your life story that you never saw coming.

Imagine this: you started off freelancing or consulting, thinking it was just a temporary gig. But suddenly, you found yourself at the helm of your own business, creating something big and exciting. It's as if you mixed some random ingredients just to see what would happen, and surprisingly, you ended up cooking up something truly amazing. Your business grows in the most unexpected ways, much like a beautiful plant sprouting in a spot where you never even planted a seed.

Now, here's your real challenge: keeping that momentum going and finding a steady rhythm. Your business model is as spontaneous as your journey, which means figuring out the next steps can feel a bit like learning to dance to a brand-new tune.

What's truly exciting about being an Accidental Hero is discovering opportunities you didn't even know existed. Maybe your content agency stumbled into social media marketing, or your web development firm started offering SEO services. It's all about finding new directions to grow and shine.

If you're nodding along thinking, "That sounds exactly like me," then you've got some incredible strengths at your disposal. You're adaptable, excellent at seizing opportunities, and skilled at rallying a team that's ready for anything.

Of course, stepping off the beaten path has its challenges. Moving forward without a traditional business plan requires creativity, smart thinking, and a dash of courage to face the unknown. It's about making the most of every surprise, turning each unexpected opportunity into a thrilling new adventure.

So, to all the budding Fatepreneurs out there, remember this: your journey might have started by accident, but it's your vision, resilience, and willingness to embrace the unexpected that will define your success.

As we dive deeper into these different paths, one thing becomes crystal clear: the road to discovery is often filled with surprises. It's not just about chance—it's about seeing those unexpected turns as opportunities for growth. Stepping out of your comfort zone becomes less about risk and more about taking a strategic leap toward innovation.

We've talked about the different journeys people take in the digital agency world, right? But there's one thing that ties them all together: that spark of inspiration. You know the moment—you're watching your favorite movie, the music swells, and suddenly, the hero has a moment of clarity. It's the moment when everything changes, and you're hooked because you know something big is about to happen.

That's exactly what it's like when you embark on your own adventure of launching a digital marketing agency. It's the point in your story where the pieces start falling into place—just like when Peter Parker discovers his spider-like powers. It's a turning point, and everything suddenly looks different.

You may ask why these flashes of brilliance are so crucial. Well, they're not just the opening scenes of your agency's story; they're the soul of it. These bursts of insight light up the path, guiding you as you make your way through the journey of building your agency from scratch.

As we embrace the significance of these defining moments, let me take you through a personal chapter from my own journey. Diving back into the thick of things, there I was, comfortable as a content consultant. It was a steady gig, a passion play—the kind that had me feeling like a behind-the-scenes wizard. But then, out of nowhere, life decided to throw in a plot twist worthy of a Bollywood blockbuster. Clients who'd seen a bit of my behind-the-curtain magic started dropping hints. "Why not take center stage?" they said. Imagine that moment in a film when the underdog suddenly finds the spotlight turned on them. And what better assurance than a paying client asking you to do more?

I began piecing together plans that felt more like sketches for a grand masterpiece. What started as doodles on napkins during coffee breaks started looking more like a blueprint for something new, something mine.

This story, while uniquely mine, isn't uncommon. It's a path trodden by dreamers and doers who dare to listen to those whispers of ambition. It's that split-second realisation, a mix of clarity and exhilaration, sparking the journey from 'what if' to 'let's do this.' Think of them as your personal bat signal, calling you to action.

Now, as we ride this wave of inspiration, let's peek into what comes next. How do we take these brilliant sparks and turn them into a model of success?

THE PASSION PLAYBOOK

Let's map out how that initial burst of passion becomes the cornerstone of a booming digital marketing agency. It's like when you have that first cup of chai in the morning—essential, but just the beginning of what's needed to kickstart your day.

Securing the very first client is a massive leap into the unknown, a leap that every digital agency founder remembers vividly. It's the first rite of passage for every digital agency founder. This isn't about simply showing off what you can do; it's about sharing a slice of your life, making it personal, like you're inviting someone to take a walk through your journey.

When I think back to landing my first client, it wasn't a straightforward pitch. No, it was more like sitting down for a chat, where I unfolded the aspects of my professional life - the ups, the downs, and everything in between. This approach was about establishing a connection, showing that reliability and trustworthiness weren't just buzzwords to me but principles I lived by. For those who were just getting to know me, this storytelling was my handshake, my promise of expertise and real, tangible results.

But here's the deal: being skilled is a fantastic start, but becoming irreplaceable? Now, that's the key. It's about zeroing in on that one unique problem only you can solve. Think of it as your signature tune in a world of noise, the kind that makes people sit up and listen, the kind that has them coming back for more. This is the moment your role shifts—from just another option in the directory to the go-to expert, the first name they think of in a bind.

This transformation is monumental. So, for anyone standing at the starting line, wondering how to make that leap, remember, it's about making it personal, diving deep to find that unique value you bring to the table, and then sharing it with the world. It's about turning your story, your journey, into the very reason they chose you. Let's not just be good at what we do; let's be unforgettable.

As we continue on this journey, it becomes evident that building your agency is as much about the people you bring on board as it is about the clients you serve.

Building a team isn't one-size-fits-all. It's about understanding the core of your agency—whether you're a Freelancing Firefly lighting up new ideas, a Lifestyle Hustler navigating the market with savvy, an MNC Monger bringing corporate strategies to the entrepreneurial table, or an Accidental Hero stumbling upon success. Each archetype demands a different strategy for assembling a dream team.

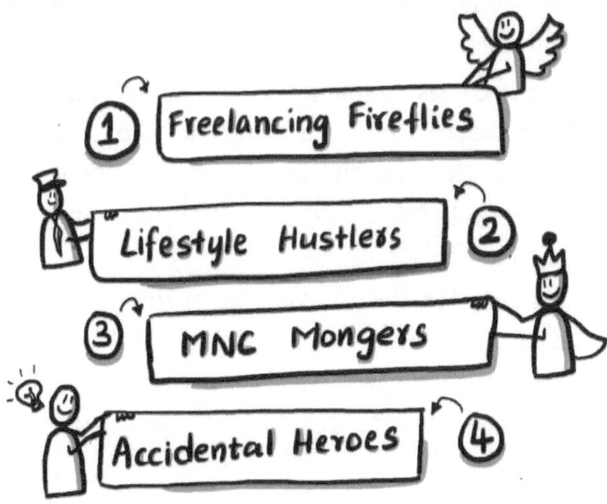

For Freelancing Fireflies: Look for versatility and self-motivation. You need folks who can wear multiple hats, adapt quickly, and are not afraid to dive into uncharted territories. Encourage ownership and autonomy, allowing them to shine and bring innovative solutions to the table.

Lifestyle Hustlers: Your focus should be on finding individuals who not only have the knack for spotting opportunities but also possess the hustle to make things happen. Emphasise on building a network-savvy team capable of leveraging contacts and turning conversations into contracts.

MNC Mongers: Seek out professionals who can appreciate the structure and predictability of corporate life but are eager to apply those skills in a more dynamic setting. Balance is key here; blend your corporate strategies with the agility and creativity needed in the agency world.

Accidental Heroes: Embrace diversity in skills and backgrounds. Since your journey into the agency space was quite unplanned, look for team members who can bring a fresh perspective, complementing your vision with their unique insights and experiences.

When it comes to finances, the approach should be as personalised and strategic as building your team. Regardless of your archetype, clear, upfront communication about payment terms is non-negotiable. Yet, how you navigate these waters can vary.

Freelancing Fireflies and Accidental Heroes might prefer more flexible payment structures initially to accommodate diverse client bases and projects. Consider phased payments or performance-based models that reflect the agile nature of your operations.

Lifestyle Hustlers, known for their knack for negotiation, should leverage their skills to secure favourable terms, ensuring cash flow consistency without compromising on the value of their services.

MNC Mongers might implement structured payment schedules that reflect their appreciation for predictability and order, mirroring more traditional business models but adapting to the digital marketing landscape.

Across all archetypes, integrating technology to manage finances—from invoicing and payments to budget tracking—can streamline operations, making it easier to keep the financial health of your agency in check. Moreover, crafting detailed contracts that outline the scope of work, deliverables, timelines, and payment schedules will safeguard your agency's interests, ensuring that both parties are aligned and expectations are clear. By customising these strategies to match your unique style, you're nurturing a living, breathing entity that's ready to succeed. But how do you make sure this all doesn't just stay as a plan on paper? How do you bring this vision to life? Well, I've got just the story for you.

GLOBAL GALLERY

The Meteoric Rise of Wieden+Kennedy

It is enlightening to look beyond our borders and glean insights from agencies around the world. Back in '82, in a quirky corner above a meatpacking warehouse in Portland, Dan Wieden and David Kennedy were cooking up something special. Now, picture Dan with his wild, storytelling flair, a bit like our Accidental Hero who stumbles upon greatness. And there's David, the detail-oriented strategist and our MNC Monger, who knows the corporate world but craves creative freedom. Together, they're the perfect mash-up of archetypes we've been chatting about, proving that when different minds collide, magic happens.

Their lightbulb flash was more like a "Holy smokes, we're onto something!" as they came together and found their agency, Wieden+Kennedy. From their first Nike commercials that aired during the 1982 New York City Marathon to winning

Emmy Awards for ads like "The Morning After" and "Move," Wieden+Kennedy created cultural phenomena. Their campaigns, including the iconic "Just Do It" tagline, resonated with the audience, stirred emotions, and became ingrained in the public consciousness.

Building their team, Dan and David looked for believers, dreamers, and doers who brought their own unique zest to the table. They created a culture where every idea was welcome and where every team member could leave their mark. This was about building a family where everyone had a stake in the game.

And when it came to finances and client relationships, they were pioneers, setting clear terms but also building partnerships based on mutual respect and shared vision. Their work with Nike was a collaboration, a perfect example of what happens when you treat clients as partners.

So, why does Wieden+Kennedy's story matter to us? It's a live demo of everything we've been talking about. It shows how tapping into your unique strengths, understanding your archetype, and how building a team that complements you can catapult you from a modest start-up to a global sensation. It's proof that with the right mix of creativity, strategy, and a bit of audacity, the sky's the limit. Watching their rise from a simple warehouse to dominating the world stage is a powerful reminder.

So, how about we dive a bit deeper into what makes us tick, what could trip us up, and the windfalls and pitfalls that lie ahead? That's right, let's sketch out a roadmap through a SWOT analysis tailored for each archetype of agency founder.

Type	Strength	Weakness	Opportunity	Threat
Freelancing Firefly	Deep niche expertise, agility, and a personal brand that connects with clients.	Possible over-reliance on personal effort, which may result in scalability problems.	To grow services and partner with freelancers or agencies for bigger projects.	Competing against bigger agencies with more resources and a wider range of services.
Lifestyle Hustler	Strong networking skills and the ability to identify and seize new trends and opportunities.	May lack expertise in specific areas required for scaling beyond a certain point.	Using business skills to expand and enter new markets.	Economic changes impact their adaptable business models.
MNC Monger	Brings a structured approach, strategic insights, and extensive corporate network.	Having trouble with the agility and flexibility needed in a startup or agency setting.	To bring creative agility and corporate efficiency together through innovative solutions.	Struggling to adapt to the fast-paced, ever-changing digital marketing landscape.
Accidental Hero	Ability to adapt quickly, often bringing fresh, unconventional approaches to the table.	No formal business structure or planning can hinder long-term growth.	To formalize and structure the business model for sustained growth from unexpected successes.	Relying too much on a handful of successful projects or clients without a clear expansion plan.

Coming right off our deep-dive SWOT analysis, it feels like we've just struck gold, doesn't it? Each archetype, with its own strengths, weaknesses, opportunities, and threats, gives us a clearer map of what lies ahead.

Here's where we strap in for the ride, amp up the hustle, and pour our hearts into the craft. And as we begin, let's hang on to these words, " *The biggest adventure you can take is to live the life of your dreams.*"

CHAPTER 2

THE NICHE ADVANTAGE

Take a moment to think about the next step of your journey. What's going to set you apart from the hundreds, if not thousands, of other agencies out there? This is where creating a niche for your digital marketing agency becomes essential.

Every service business has its own unique identity, something that makes it click. Think of your business's niche as its Patronus—the embodiment of everything it stands for and excels at. The Patronus, for those unfamiliar, is like a powerful spirit animal, symbolizing the strengths and specialties that define you. Your business's Patronus is what clients will recognize, trust, and rely on. And just like in the wizarding world, your Patronus will keep away the Dementors of redundancy, ensuring your brand stays fresh, distinct, and irreplaceable in a crowded market.

To truly harness the power of your agency's Patronus, it's essential to understand the value of specialization. Instead of trying to be a jack-of-all-trades, narrowing your focus allows you to excel and stand out in a crowded market. Recent research from Databox shows that 77.27per cent of digital marketing agencies surveyed are zeroing in on a niche—and for good reason. Specializing makes your business the go-to choice when clients are looking for expertise in a particular area. It's far easier to be recognized for doing one thing exceptionally well than to risk blending into the crowd by trying to be everything for everyone.

Offering a broad range of services might seem like a good way to attract clients, but it's easy to become just another option.

When you focus on a niche, you give your agency clarity. Your expertise becomes sharper, and your voice becomes louder. Clients searching for exactly what you do will find you, and that's where the magic happens.

But here's the reality: the concept of specialization isn't exactly new. It's been brewing over time, picking up steam as digital strategies have progressed. Back in the early 2000s, things started shifting when analytics and digital ad platforms became more refined. Marketers realized they didn't need to speak to everyone; they could focus on segments of an audience and get far better results. This shift marked the beginning of a new way of thinking.

By the time we hit the 2010s, terms like "niche" had evolved from mere buzzwords into actual strategies. As content marketing and SEO developed, specializing meant being able to connect with the right clients, the ones who actually needed what you were offering.

Fast forward to today, and we're living in a world where the number of marketing channels has exploded, and competition is fierce. Standing out is no longer a luxury; it's a necessity. It gives you an edge in a crowded space, helping you rise above the noise and make your mark.

THE NICHE FORMULA

So, how do you stand out? It all starts with finding the right niche. I know that choosing your agency's niche can feel like a daunting task. The pressure of making the "right" decision can weigh heavily, but that's exactly why I've developed The Niche Formula—a practical guide for agency founders to make this decision less overwhelming. Let's break it down step by step.

Passion + Expertise

It all begins with two things: passion and expertise. These are the key points for figuring out your agency's niche. Why? Because a lot of successful agencies are built on the strengths and experiences of their founders. It's common for agency founders to mold their initial services around their own professional journeys. Think about it—if you've spent years perfecting the art of SEO or web development, wouldn't it make sense to shape your agency around those skills? Or, if your background is in lead generation, performance marketing could naturally become your agency's focus. Similarly, if you thrive on creativity, branding and design could be your sweet spot.

In my own case, I found a niche by combining content creation with strategic planning. These were areas where I had the expertise and enjoyed the work. This combination allowed me to offer quick-turnaround content solutions with long-lasting impact, positioning my agency as a go-to for both short-term wins and long-term strategy. The takeaway here is that your niche should showcase what you're good at, but it should also give you control over the quality and outcomes of your work. That's where passion and expertise intersect.

GAUGING MARKET DEMAND

Once you've zeroed in on your expertise, the next step is to gauge the market demand. This is where some research comes into play. You'll want to dig into market trends and understand where your services might be most needed. Is there a demand for the services you want to offer? Let's say you find that B2B SaaS companies are on the lookout for tailored content marketing strategies—this could be your golden ticket to establishing a focused niche. By understanding these market dynamics, you'll ensure there's a strong demand for your services, which is key for long-term growth.

Who Are Your Target Audience?

Understanding who needs your services is the next piece of the puzzle. If you're eyeing the tech startup space for branding services, get to know these companies intimately. What challenges do they face? What goals are they striving to achieve? This understanding allows you to tailor your services so precisely that your agency becomes the obvious choice for those in the know.

UNDERSTANDING COMPETITION

Understanding who you're up against is crucial. Take a moment to think about how crowded your intended niche is. A packed market signals strong demand, but it also means standing out could be a challenge. Your job is to carve out a space that's uniquely yours.

For example, SEO services are everywhere, but what if you specialize in e-commerce SEO? Suddenly, you're not competing with everyone. You're zooming in on a very specific group: online businesses that face unique challenges in getting their products found. This is where you can make your agency indispensable by focusing on the exact pain points e-commerce brands deal with—like product visibility or cart abandonment. The question to ask is, how can your agency offer solutions that others aren't even thinking about?

EVALUATING PROFITABILITY

Next, let's talk about profitability. A niche might seem popular, but is it actually profitable? You'll need to dig a little deeper to understand the financial potential of your chosen area. For instance, in lead generation for real estate agents, the stakes are high. The value of a single sale in real estate is significant, which means that offering specialized services to this group can result in high-ticket projects. And that's the sweet spot—focusing on a niche where your services hold real, measurable value.

STAYING INFORMED ON INDUSTRY TRENDS

But it doesn't stop there. Keeping up with industry trends is key to staying relevant. If you're working in website development, you know that mobile optimization has become a must. Clients aren't just looking for basic websites—they need designs that perform seamlessly on mobile devices. This kind of knowledge sets you apart. When you stay on top of trends and anticipate what's next, you position your agency as the one that's always a step ahead.

Evaluating Scalability

Then, think about scalability. Sure, you might start small with a niche like organic marketing for wellness brands, but is there room to grow? Can you expand your services as the industry evolves? That's the beauty of selecting a niche with scalability - it ensures that your agency can evolve without losing its identity.

Resource Availability

As you refine your niche, it's essential to take stock of what your agency already excels at. Think about your team's strengths. If you've got a crew of top-tier content creators and designers, it makes perfect sense to lean into content marketing. This is about working smart—leveraging the skills you have to make an impact in your chosen niche. Ask yourself: does the niche align with what your team is best at? If the answer is a confident yes, you're already halfway there. Aligning your team's talents with the niche's demands is how you set yourself up for success right from the start.

REGULATORY CONSIDERATIONS

Once you've narrowed down your niche, there's another piece of the puzzle to fit—regulatory considerations. These are more than just a checklist; they're essential to keeping both your agency and your clients in the clear. Take healthcare marketing as an example. If your niche involves building websites for medical professionals, you'll need to ensure your work complies with HIPAA regulations. This is a vital step in building trust with your clients and avoiding legal pitfalls.

Let's understand how each part of the formula we've talked about fits together:

(Passion + Expertise) x Market Demand ÷ Competition + (Target Audience Insights + Profit Potential) + Industry Trends x Scalability – Resource Gaps + Regulatory Compliance = Your Perfect Niche

It sounds like a mouthful, but trust me, this formula works. It takes everything we've discussed—your passions, your team's strengths, market demand, competition, profitability, and even regulations—and wraps them into one neat package. This formula is a way to ensure your niche isn't just something you stumble upon but something you actively craft.

Finding the Robin to Your Batman

By now, you've got a solid foundation in identifying your niche, using the formula to validate your direction. Once your niche is locked in, the next step is thinking about how to round out your offerings with complementary services that can enhance your core strengths. These additional services might not demand your full attention, but they play a critical role in your agency's long-term success.

As you hone in on your niche, it's important to think about how supporting services can align with your main offering. These services add value to what you already do and create new opportunities to generate revenue. Consider it like this: your niche is like Batman. It's the service that takes the spotlight and leads the way. But every Batman needs a Robin, right? That supporting service might not be in the spotlight, but it's essential in keeping the whole operation running smoothly. These are the services that can often be delegated to your team, allowing you to focus on your core offering while ensuring a steady revenue stream. They're also the ones that can be bundled with your primary service to create a more comprehensive solution for clients. This means you're providing your clients with plenty of reasons to stick with you for the long run, all while boosting your profits.

When expanding your niche to include these supporting services, consider how forward or backward integration could benefit your agency. Let's say your speciality is website development. A logical next step might be to add SEO services. Website development brings in an initial surge of revenue, but SEO services ensure that the client remains engaged through ongoing retainers, creating a longer-term partnership. This strategic pairing can help strengthen client relationships while offering all-inclusive solutions that keep them coming back.

Similarly, if your agency shines in content writing, why stop there? Pairing content creation with branding and design services can elevate your offerings from a single project to a full-service package. This approach makes your workflow more efficient and allows your clients to build a cohesive brand narrative across all their campaigns. In today's competitive digital world, agencies that can handle everything—from crafting engaging content to overseeing the entire brand identity—are the ones that truly stand out.

You might also want to think about adding services that don't require heavy lifting but still bring in significant returns. Services like social listening, reputation management, and lead generation are becoming essential in a market driven by digital interactions. These services are perfect complements to more intensive tasks, such as managing social media, because they give you key insights into market trends and consumer behavior. With this information, your agency can deliver data-driven results without overextending its resources.

Choosing the right support services to complement your niche can do wonders, much like how Robin complements Batman, ensuring that every mission is a success. This strategic approach enhances your ability to fully serve your clients and cements your status as a versatile, niche expert in the digital marketing world.

NICHE REVENUE FRAMEWORK

Once you've defined your niche and paired it with complementary services, the next challenge is figuring out how to monetize it effectively. It's one thing to carve out a specialized space for your agency, but making that niche profitable requires a carefully thought-out strategy. Financial considerations are crucial here. While niche markets often offer higher margins due to specialization, they can also mean less volume of work, which makes it even more important to have a solid revenue plan in place.

From my own experience and from conversations with talented peers in the industry, I've realized that monetizing a niche is tricky. It's not just about knowing your niche but understanding how to navigate it financially. I've created a framework from my experience that has really helped me successfully monetize the niche of my digital marketing agency.

The first step in this framework is ***In-Depth Market Research***. Start by diving deep into the market you've chosen. In today's rapidly changing environment, it's not enough to follow trends—you need to anticipate them. Using advanced research tools, like big data analytics and AI, can give you a real advantage. These tools help you spot emerging patterns, understand shifts in consumer behavior, and predict where the market is heading.

But that's just part of it. You'll also need to conduct ***a gap analysis*** to figure out what's missing in your niche. What needs are going unmet? What areas are underserved? By finding these gaps, you create opportunities for your agency to step in and offer something truly valuable. It's all about identifying where you can fill a void and meet a demand that others aren't addressing.

In my own journey, comprehensive market research was crucial in spotting lucrative trends in the edutech and healthtech sectors, particularly in urban hubs like Bangalore, Mumbai, and Hyderabad. We noticed that digital marketing services tailored to these industries were lacking, and by filling this gap, we positioned our agency as the go-to solution. Our passion for storytelling and brand building in these sectors allowed us to deliver exceptional value, which helped us stand out from the competition and command premium pricing for our specialized services.

The next part of this framework is all about ***diversification and adaptability***. While specialization makes you an expert, having a diverse range of services keeps your agency agile and better prepared for market changes.

By diversifying strategically, you ensure that your agency isn't too dependent on a single stream of income. Maintaining a broad portfolio allows you to balance your niche expertise with other market opportunities. This way, even if there are fluctuations in your niche, you can still capitalize on emerging trends without feeling vulnerable to market shifts. It's about finding the right mix that helps you stay relevant across different client needs while still leveraging your specialization.

Another important element of this is ***customization***. Developing service packages that are flexible enough to cater to different client segments within your niche can make all the difference. By offering tailored solutions, you're able to attract a broader range of clients, each with unique needs, and increase the appeal of your agency. This flexibility expands your client base and reinforces your niche's strength by ensuring you're meeting various demands without stretching too thin.

For me, maintaining a diverse portfolio has been key to monetizing our niche. It allowed us to take on different challenges, keeping things fresh and motivating the team. Having a variety of services also meant that we could adjust quickly when new opportunities arose, ensuring we stayed ahead of the game. This adaptability has been crucial for our sustained growth, making sure we didn't get stuck in one place but kept evolving as the market did.

Another essential aspect of the framework is ***positioning your agency as a thought leader in your niche.*** Establishing your expertise sets you apart from the competition and builds trust with potential clients. Thought leadership is about showing, not just telling, that your agency knows its stuff.

One of the most effective ways to do this is through content-driven thought leadership. Creating and sharing high-quality content that demonstrates your insights into your niche is key. Whether it's through publishing detailed white papers, hosting webinars, or even speaking at industry events, each piece of content you put out there builds credibility. It shows that you understand the challenges of your niche and that you have the solutions to offer.

But thought leadership doesn't stop at content. ***Engaging with your community*** is just as important. By participating in industry forums, online communities, and social media platforms, you can connect with peers and potential clients alike. This kind of active engagement builds your agency's reputation as a key player in the field. Plus, it's a great way to attract new business—people are far more likely to work with an agency that they see as influential and engaged in their industry.

When I was just starting out, breaking into the world of big brands felt like a steep uphill climb. Without an established portfolio, it was tough to get a foot in the door. But my background as a business journalist gave me a unique insight: while many agencies were chasing large corporates, there was a huge opportunity in serving small and medium-sized enterprises (SMEs). These businesses were often overlooked, but they were eager for growth and open to innovation. By focusing on this niche, we built a strong reputation in a less crowded space, which in turn helped us create a portfolio that eventually attracted bigger clients.

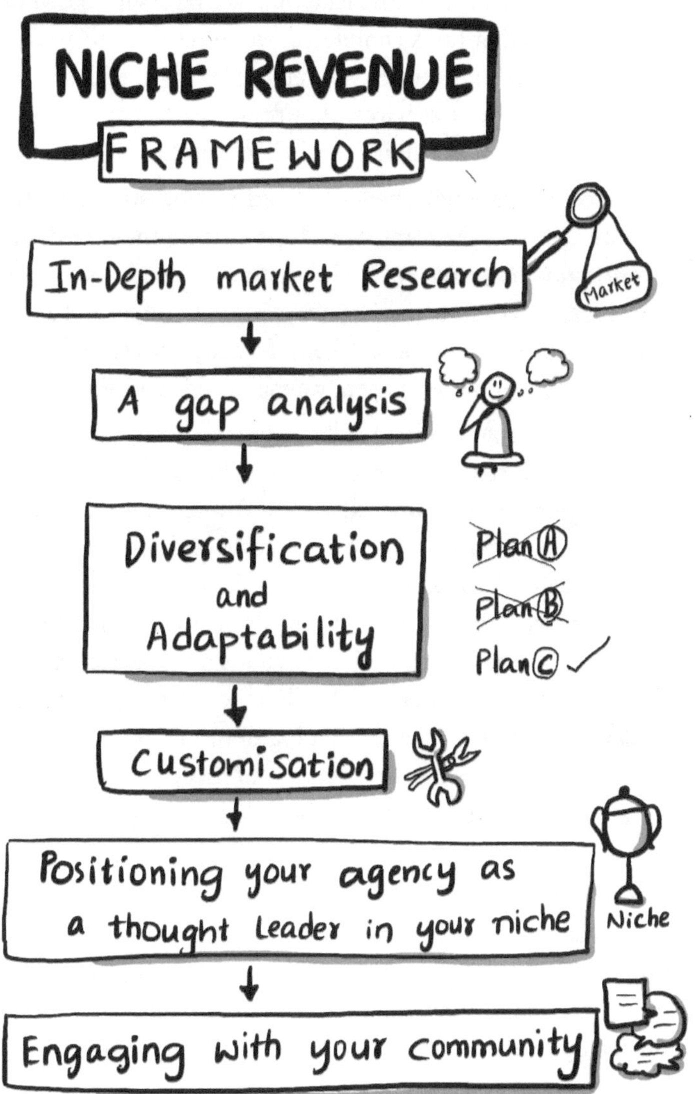

Of course, positioning your agency as a thought leader is just one part of the equation. Another crucial step is implementing ***advanced pricing strategies*** that reflect the value you bring to the table. Value-based pricing is one approach that has worked wonders for us. Instead of charging clients based on the hours worked or tasks completed, we structured our pricing around the value and results we deliver. When clients see the direct benefits of your services, they're willing to pay for those outcomes—and that can significantly boost profitability.

Once you've established advanced pricing strategies, the next critical step in the framework is ***leveraging client feedback for continuous improvement***. No matter how well your niche services are performing, there's always room to refine and adapt based on real-world results. Client feedback becomes a key driver in shaping how your agency evolves and stays ahead.

It's important to gather feedback systematically. After every project, create a structured process that allows clients to share their thoughts on what worked well and where improvements can be made. This can be done through surveys, direct interviews, or simple feedback forms that capture detailed insights. The real value comes when you analyze this feedback to fuel innovation. Identifying patterns in the challenges your clients face or hearing about unfulfilled needs opens the door to new opportunities. This data can guide you in developing new services or refining your current offerings to better serve your niche.

Client feedback played a major role in our agency's growth. We worked with direct-to-consumer artisanal brands in cities like Jaipur and Udaipur, and consistently delivering strong results gave us insight into emerging niche markets like eCommerce, healthtech, and education. The feedback loop was instrumental in helping us identify gaps and refine our approach. This process validated our expertise, further cementing our reputation within these specialized sectors.

Following this niche revenue framework, you'll be well on your way to turning your niche services into a thriving, profitable business. It's a strategic approach that helps you grow sustainably and gives you a clear niche advantage in the marketplace.

GLOBAL GALLERY

Finding the Niche: Where Big Spaceship Took Off

To better understand how the concepts of the Niche Formula and the Niche Revenue Framework come to life in successful agencies, let's take a look at Big Spaceship, a digital marketing agency based in Brooklyn, New York. This agency has become a leader in the digital creative industry, working with big names like Google, Starbucks, and JetBlue. Their journey offers valuable insights into how they applied niche-focused strategies to carve out their space in a highly competitive field.

Big Spaceship's story began in the early 2000s, a time when digital media was starting to reshape the marketing world. The agency decided to focus on the movie industry, providing creative digital solutions for companies like Sony Pictures and Miramax Films. This early specialization gave Big Spaceship a reputation for being experts in digital storytelling—a perfect example of the Niche Formula in action. By combining their passion for digital media with their expertise, they aligned themselves with a growing market need, setting themselves up for long-term success.

The agency's founders, Michael Lebowitz and Daniel Federman, had a deep-rooted passion for digital media and storytelling. This became the foundation of Big Spaceship's niche. Their unique take on digital storytelling is what we could call their "Patronus," representing the core strengths and specialties that allowed them to stand out in the market. By focusing on creativity and innovation, they positioned themselves as leaders in the digital space, delivering solutions that were both cutting-edge and impactful.

Big Spaceship also knew how to gauge market demand. They recognized that more and more brands were looking for ways to engage with audiences on digital platforms. By identifying this growing need early on, they were able to offer exactly what these brands were searching for—further solidifying their niche in the industry.

Big Spaceship's ability to attract and retain major clients like Google, Starbucks, and JetBlue is no accident. By honing in on digital storytelling and user engagement, Big Spaceship has consistently provided value through specialized services that meet the unique needs of these high-profile clients.

At the core of their success is a client-centric approach. Big Spaceship understands that delivering exceptional results isn't just about offering great services—it's about tailoring those services to fit each client's specific goals. Their niche specialization allowed them to focus on digital storytelling, but it was their commitment to understanding each client's unique challenges and needs that helped them build lasting partnerships. This focus on customization and innovation has made them a trusted partner for some of the world's biggest brands.

There's a lot to learn from Big Spaceship's journey. First, their dedication to niche specialization shows the power of focusing on a specific area of expertise to stand out from the competition. They became leaders in digital storytelling by staying true to their strengths and offering something distinct in a crowded market.

Next, their innovative culture played a huge role in keeping the agency at the forefront of the industry. Fostering creativity and collaboration among teams has allowed Big Spaceship to consistently come up with fresh, effective solutions for their clients. It's this spirit of innovation that keeps them relevant and helps them deliver standout results, time and again.

Finally, their strategic engagement with clients highlights the importance of understanding and addressing specific needs. Big Spaceship's ability to listen closely to what their clients are looking for, and then tailor solutions to meet those needs, has been critical in building strong, long-term relationships that lead to sustained growth.

Big Spaceship's journey shows how staying true to a specific area of expertise and continuously evolving with market demands can lead to long-term growth and success in even the most competitive industries.

In the journey of growing your agency, there's always more beneath the surface than meets the eye. As you've seen from Big Spaceship's example, finding your niche and creating a revenue framework is an ongoing process that demands adaptability, foresight, and a commitment to staying relevant.

Your journey is alive, evolving, and ultimately defined by the actions you take. So, take a moment to reflect on where your agency stands today, and more importantly, where you want it to go tomorrow.

CHAPTER 3

MORE THAN A NAME TAG

Ever noticed what ancient cave paintings and today's blockbuster movies have in common? You are correct if you find yourself mouthing the word 'stories'. Stories have been shaping us for ages. We humans are naturally wired to be drawn to stories. They stir up our emotions, spark our interest, and somehow, make us feel more connected. Whether it's a tale from thousands of years ago or a modern-day film, the essence of storytelling remains the same - to captivate and connect. Similarly, the world of branding revolves around stories that stick with us long after we've encountered them. Arianna Huffington, co-founder of The Huffington Post, hit the nail on the head when she said, *"People think in stories, not statistics, and marketers need to be master storytellers."*

Sure, facts and figures might catch our eye, but a great story? Now, that's something we don't easily forget. When it comes to your digital marketing agency, telling a compelling brand story is key to being remembered and staying on the potential clients' radar. It's all about turning those just-browsing visitors into loyal customers who come back for more and bring their friends along.

THE CORNERSTONE OF YOUR BRAND STORY

In the journey of telling your brand's story, creating a compelling brand identity is the crucial first step. It's more than just a cool logo or a snappy catchphrase. It's about setting up a solid base that really shows off who you are and what you're all about. To get that foundation right, there are three big principles every agency needs to nail: being clear, staying consistent, and keeping it real.

Crystal Clear Identity

First, let's talk about clarity. Your brand identity should clearly communicate who you are, what you believe in, and what sets you apart from the competition. It's like having a well-defined plot in a story—without it, your audience won't understand your message. When you define your core values, mission, and unique selling propositions right from the start, you give your audience a clear and compelling reason to choose you.

CONSISTENT CHARACTER

Next is consistency. Think of it as the rhythm in your story that keeps everything in sync. Your brand should look, feel, and sound the same across all platforms, whether it's your website, social media, or marketing materials. This consistent presence builds trust and makes your brand instantly recognizable. When people see your logo or read your content, they should immediately know it's you. This familiarity is what turns casual visitors into loyal clients.

Genuine Vibes Only

Finally, authenticity is what makes your brand story real and relatable. It's about being genuine and true to your values in every interaction. Authenticity resonates with people because it inspires trust and creates a deeper emotional connection. When your brand reflects who you genuinely are, it attracts clients who share your values and builds long-term relationships.

With clarity, consistency, and authenticity at the core of your brand identity, differentiating your agency becomes a natural process. It's all about turning what might seem like the same old services into something uniquely you, and carving your own special niche in the industry. For instance, if your agency specializes in eco-friendly brands, every aspect of your branding from the visuals to the message should reinforce your commitment to sustainability. This clear and consistent focus attracts clients who share your values and strengthens your position as a leader in this niche.

You've got the basics of creating a unique brand identity for your agency down pat. Now, let's tackle the next important step with an exercise. Think about Apple or Nike for a moment. Close your eyes and picture either brand. What comes to mind? Maybe it's the sleek design of an iPhone or the iconic Nike swoosh. This exercise highlights how powerful a brand's visual language can be. It's direct, memorable, and manages to feel both natural and unique.

Now, let's dive into crafting a visual language for your brand. This is all about turning your brand identity into engaging visuals that grab attention and resonate deeply with your audience. Here's how you can make it all come together.

Picture Your People

Let's start with getting to know your audience. What visuals draw them in? Are they moved by bold, vibrant colors, or do they prefer more subdued, classic styles? Understanding these preferences is crucial because your visual language needs to resonate with them directly. For instance, if your audience leans towards youthful and energetic, splash those bright colors and dynamic shapes across your designs. But if they value tradition, opt for timeless fonts and a conservative color palette.

Brand Harmony

Embrace consistency to ensure harmony across your brand. It's crucial that your colors, typography, and design style are uniformly presented, no matter the platform. This uniformity helps cement your brand identity in the minds of your audience. Whether they're browsing your website, glancing at your social media, or opening an email from you, they should immediately recognize it's from your brand.

Tug Those Heartstrings

Visuals are more than just pretty designs; they're the heartstring tuggers. The right images and design elements can stir up emotions, helping forge a deeper connection with your audience. Think about the emotions you want to evoke. Is it trust? Excitement? Inspiration? Choose visuals that reflect these feelings. This emotional resonance enhances your brand's appeal and helps you forge a stronger bond with your audience.

Flexibility is Your Friend

Your visual language should work everywhere—from your digital ads to print materials, from social media to in-person events. This versatility ensures that your brand remains cohesive and recognizable, no matter the medium. Your logo, colors, and fonts need to shine everywhere, whether it's on a tiny business card or a huge billboard.

The Feedback Effect

Never underestimate the power of feedback. What does your audience think about your visual identity? Is it hitting the mark? Regularly collecting and acting on feedback is vital for refining your visual language. Keep the lines of communication open with your clients and followers. Their insights will help you tweak and improve your visuals, ensuring they always resonate with your target audience.

Creating a compelling brand identity and visual language is about more than just looking good—it's about making meaningful connections. Done right, it acts as a magnet, drawing in your ideal clients and distinguishing you in a crowded digital marketing space.

THE BRAND JOURNAL

As we explore the different aspects of your brand's story and identity, I'd like to share a key moment from my own journey that really underscored how crucial visual identity is for our agency.

You know, one of those "aha" moments in our journey toward crafting a unique brand identity? That was the story behind our brand logo and identity. It's quite a tale, especially how it all came together when we boldly stepped into the digital world.

It took three months of non-stop brainstorming marathons, sketching out designs, and making more revisions than we could count. It was a road dotted with setbacks and outright rejections. We played around with all sorts of taglines, logos, and visual styles, trying to find the perfect fit. There were moments when the frustration got so real, we'd just snap—in a throwback to the days of old-school brainstorming, we'd crumple up our designs and toss them into the bin, all because they didn't quite nail what we were about.

So there we were, another late night at the office, surrounded by heaps of tossed aside ideas and the weight of deadlines looming over us. We were sifting through the chaos, and that's when it happened. We stumbled upon a crumpled piece of paper. Now, this wasn't just any piece of paper. As we smoothed it out, something just clicked. It was like a eureka moment, you know?

This crumpled paper was going to be our background. It was like it breathed a whole new life into our design. It perfectly captured everything we wanted to say, aligning flawlessly with our vision and values. It was our eureka moment, and you could feel the energy shift in the room. Everyone felt it. From the second we chose that crinkled paper look for our background, it turned into a badge of honor, showing off our grit, our wild ideas, and just how real we were. That choice shaped our brand's identity for an amazing seven years.

We stumbled upon this quirky visual - a crushed paper background. It was different, it was us, and just like that, it became the heart of our brand's identity.

Reflecting on our branding journey, let's unpack some lessons that might light up your own path to a standout brand identity.

Keep It Real with Your Story: Think about what makes your brand special. It's more than your logo or colors. It's about your story. For us, it was all about a unique crushed paper background that really showed off our resilience and creativity. This choice was a reflection of our journey, our challenges, and our wins. That realness really resonated with our audience, helping us build connections that go way beyond the usual customer-business stuff.

Trial and Error, But Keep Going: Creating our brand identity felt like running a marathon, not dashing through a sprint. We rode the rollercoaster of trials, errors, and those lightbulb moments. Every piece of feedback, even the rejections, pushed us closer to finding a brand identity that genuinely felt like us. Sure, the process got a bit messy at times. But you know what? That's where the real magic is — sticking to it, changing things up, and coming out stronger on the other side.

Innovate Like You Mean It: When we switched gears to focus more on digital, adding our signature crushed paper texture into our digital designs, it was more than just following the crowd. We were aiming to set a new bar, proving that we could be leaders online. This change showed everyone our knack for innovation and our readiness to embrace change, which are key traits of a brand that's always looking ahead.

GLOBAL GALLERY

Pentagram's Mastery in Branding

Let's pause for a moment to look at a global example that truly brings to life the principles we've been discussing. Pentagram, one of the world's leading design firms, has shaped iconic visual identities for countless brands while mastering the art of storytelling through design.

First, let's talk about Pentagram's own visual identity. Their logo, a powerful geometric pentagram, reflects their commitment to clarity and precision. The minimalist black-and-white palette allows their work to shine without distractions. This approach ensures that their identity remains timeless and versatile, consistently reinforcing their reputation for sophistication and excellence across all platforms.

When Reddit approached Pentagram, they faced a challenge: unifying the platform's eclectic brand elements into a cohesive identity while preserving its unique, quirky spirit. Reddit's diverse and vibrant community is its strength, and Pentagram's task was to create a visual identity that captured this energy and made it unmistakably Reddit.

One of the standout elements of the rebrand was the evolution of Reddit's mascot, Snoo. Pentagram transformed Snoo from a flat, 2D icon into a lively 3D character, aiming to make it as iconic and instantly recognizable as Super Mario. This change was about reinforcing Reddit's playful and eclectic nature, making Snoo a symbol that users could connect with on a deeper level.

Pentagram also refined Reddit's color palette, simplifying it from over 100 colors to 15 bold, vibrant hues like magenta, orange, and neon green. This reduction made Reddit's identity more cohesive and instantly recognizable.

By focusing on impactful colors, Pentagram ensured that every visual element of Reddit was connected, creating a stronger and more unified brand presence.

The custom typeface, Reddit Display, played a crucial role in the rebrand. Incorporating Reddit's signature bubble motif into the design, this typeface provided consistency across all platforms, enhancing recognition and connection with users.

Pentagram introduced the conversation bubble as a new visual element, framing text and images across Reddit's platforms. This design choice symbolizes Reddit's core focus on dialogue and community interaction, highlighting what makes Reddit special—genuine conversations that matter.

Throughout the rebranding process, Pentagram's strategic approach remained clear: preserve Reddit's core traits—its eclecticism, positivity, delightful absurdity, and candidness—while refining its brand positioning. The goal was to solidify Reddit's identity as "the heart of the internet," a hub where real conversations happen, and communities thrive.

Pentagram's work with Reddit showcases how a well-crafted visual identity, grounded in clarity, consistency, and authenticity, can elevate a brand to new heights. Pentagram didn't simply create a new look for Reddit; they crafted a story that resonates deeply with its audience, turning a digital platform into a brand with heart, character, and lasting impact.

MEASURING YOUR BRAND'S PULSE

As you dive into shaping your brand identity, including all the visual bits, it's time to take a good look at how your digital marketing agency's brand looks and feels to the outside world. This step is super important if you want to keep the success train rolling. You'll want to keep tabs on a bunch of different things and listen to what people are saying. Here's a rundown of some key metrics and ways to collect feedback that you should think about:

Name Drop or Not?: How well does your target audience recognize and remember your brand? You can measure this through surveys, focus groups, or by tracking social media mentions and direct inquiries about your brand. If people can recall your brand easily and associate it with positive attributes, you're on the right track. For example, conducting a simple survey asking people what comes to mind when they think of your brand can provide valuable insights into your brand's impact.

Digital Footprint Check: Tools like Google Analytics are invaluable for understanding how engaging and effective your website's visual and narrative elements are. Pay attention to metrics such as bounce rate, time on site, and pages per session. If visitors are staying longer and exploring more pages, it means your content is resonating with them. Additionally, track which pages are most visited and analyze what makes them successful. This can help you replicate that success across other parts of your website.

The Social Pulse: Look at likes, shares, comments, and click-through rates on social media platforms. High engagement rates indicate that your visual and narrative content resonates with your audience and encourages interaction. To deepen your understanding, consider the types of content that drive the most engagement. Are videos performing better than images? Are certain topics generating more discussion? Use this data to refine your content strategy and enhance your brand's presence on social media.

Making the Clicks Count: Conversion metrics, such as conversion rate per landing page, email sign-ups, or sales generated through digital campaigns, are crucial indicators of how effective your brand identity is. An effective brand should lead to higher conversion rates by conveying trust and credibility. For instance, if a specific landing page has a high conversion rate, analyze its design and messaging to understand what works. Then, apply those insights to other campaigns and landing pages to improve overall performance.

Reading the Room: Dive into what people are saying about your brand online. Utilizing social listening tools and sentiment analysis can reveal the overall mood and opinions surrounding your brand. A positive sentiment means people feel good about your brand, which is a strong endorsement of your visual and narrative identity.

The Honest Mirror: Direct feedback is gold. Encourage your customers to leave reviews on platforms like Google My Business and Yelp, or through industry-specific review sites. Analyze this feedback to understand how your brand influences their perceptions and decisions. It's direct insight into what you're doing right and what might need tweaking.

Keeping an Eye on the Competition: Don't operate in a bubble. Look at your competitors—what are they doing, how are they perceived, and what visual styles are they employing? This can spotlight areas for differentiation and highlight opportunities to stand out in your industry.

Testing the Waters: Here's where the rubber meets the road. Test different visual elements, messaging, or designs to see what resonates most with your audience. Which version drives more engagement or conversions? This data-driven approach will fine-tune your brand identity, ensuring it's as effective as possible.

Big-Picture Branding: Keep an eye on the bigger picture. Metrics like brand awareness, loyalty, and equity paint a picture of your brand's long-term health and resonance with your audience. These indicators help you gauge the enduring strength of your brand identity.

Regularly reviewing these metrics and adjusting based on feedback helps keep your brand relevant and ahead of the competition. It involves being flexible and responsive in a quickly changing digital world, making sure your brand keeps connecting and engaging with your audience effectively.

ENSURING YOUR BRAND STAYS RELEVANT

When you're working on strengthening your brand identity, just know it's not all smooth sailing. Let me share a bit from my own experience. While we were shaping our agency's brand, we definitely hit some bumps. Trying to juggle this with our demanding client workload was quite the adventure. Honestly, the biggest challenge we faced was balancing time and resources to focus on our branding while still keeping clients happy and the money flowing in. It's like trying to balance plates on sticks—you want your brand to shine and stay relevant, but you can't let that distract you from what's keeping the lights on.

So, here's what I did: I decided to hand over the reins of our branding efforts to our amazing team. It was like flipping a switch. Suddenly, everyone was bringing their A-game, infusing our agency's identity with all sorts of creative ideas and fresh perspectives. It was about tapping into the incredible pool of talent we had. And let me tell you, watching them take ownership and run with it was both a relief and a real eye-opener. It goes to show, sometimes, letting go a little can bring in a whole lot more than you expected—more innovation, more engagement, and a brand identity that truly reflects who we are.

We decided to try something a bit different for our Digital Ozone branding at the agency. We let our team members run free with their ideas, giving them the space to be their creative selves. It was like telling them, "Hey, there's no box!" This freedom led them to play around with new concepts and visual styles that we hadn't even thought of before. Sure, some of our ideas weren't exactly what you'd call "corporate-friendly," but they were just what we needed to spice up our agency's online vibe. These out-of-the-box ideas boosted our digital presence, got more people talking about us organically, and really connected with our target crowd.

This strategy continued to sparked a sense of ownership and pride that you could feel buzzing through the office. Everyone was more connected, more motivated—like we were all pulling together towards something big.

Before long, our clients started to really get what we were all about. They saw the spark in our innovative methods and that built a trust like no other. It was like we were all part of a team, working together to create something amazing. This teamwork fueled our growth and set us apart in a crowded market. Every success felt like a shared victory, and that's something special.

THE RELEVANCE METER

Drawing from my own rollercoaster of ups and downs, I'm excited to introduce the Relevance Meter—a tool designed to help gauge how well your agency's brand is staying relevant in the ever-evolving digital marketing landscape. Here are some nuggets of wisdom that might just keep your Relevance Meter dialed in and make your journey a bit smoother:

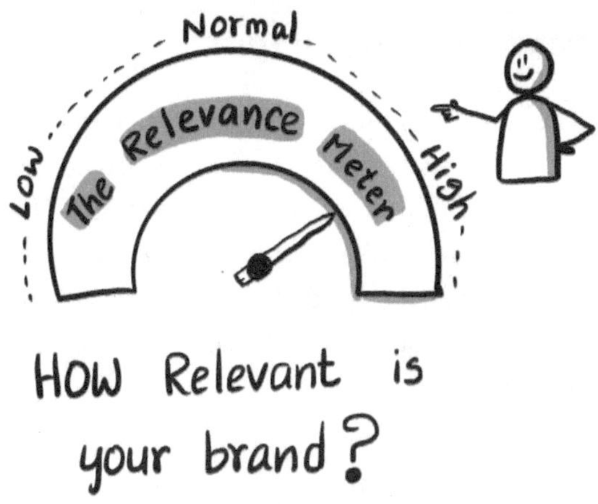

Ownership as Fuel for Relevance

Giving your team ownership of the branding process is essential for keeping your brand relevant. When your team feels invested, they're more likely to infuse fresh ideas that resonate with your audience. By seeing their own creativity come to life, they'll be inspired to keep the brand current and dynamic, ensuring it evolves naturally alongside market trends. Ownership sparks pride, and that pride fuels a brand that never feels stale.

Innovation as Your Brand's Pulse

Encouraging a culture of creativity keeps your brand innovative. The more you welcome diverse perspectives, the more you ignite new ideas that set your agency apart. When your brand consistently brings fresh, out-of-the-box solutions to the table, clients notice. And when they see that you're pushing boundaries, trust deepens, and your relevance meter skyrockets. Innovation is like the heartbeat of your brand—if it's strong, everything else falls into place.

Connection as the Driver of Trust

Relevance also depends on how deeply you connect with your clients. When your team is passionate and engaged, that energy is contagious—it spills over into client interactions. This passion strengthens trust and builds deeper connections, which leads to long-term relationships and shared victories. A brand that radiates enthusiasm stays relevant because it creates a lasting emotional connection.

Growth as the Long Game

Sustainable growth is the ultimate goal of any agency, and your brand is a key player in making that happen. Balancing branding with client work demonstrates that you're in it for the long haul. Your brand is a signal that you're building for the future, staying adaptable, and leading with foresight. This sustainable approach keeps your agency relevant as the industry evolves.

Each of these elements—ownership, innovation, connection, and growth—are the key metrics on your Relevance Meter. Keep them in check, and your brand will adapt and flourish, even as the digital marketing world shifts around you.

As you tackle the challenges ahead, the key is to keep evolving while staying relevant. It's about staying true to your brand's core but always finding fresh, creative ways to connect with new audiences and markets.

Start by truly understanding your brand—like you would a close friend. This deep connection allows you to evolve without losing what makes your brand unique. Then, dive into market research with curiosity. Learn what your target audience likes, how they behave, and what they expect. These insights let you adjust your brand's voice and appearance to resonate with them, while still keeping the essence of who you are intact.

For instance, if you're reaching out to a younger audience, consider tweaking the colors, fonts, and tone of your content to match their vibe. Create a look and feel that speaks their language, resonates with their interests, and grabs their attention. But remember, it's not just about looks—when you're pitching to new clients, focus on how your brand can meet their specific needs. Show them the value you bring by solving their problems or fulfilling their desires. By constantly evolving and staying relevant, you ensure your brand remains engaging and impactful, no matter how the market shifts.

EXPANDING YOUR BRAND'S REACH

As you work through the twists and turns of evolving your brand, the key is to find the right mix of staying true to your roots while getting creative, especially when you're trying to connect with new crowds or break into new markets. Think of it like mixing tradition with innovation—you want to maintain the authentic essence while introducing new elements that appeal to modern tastes. Start by understanding your current brand identity. Then, conduct thorough market research to grasp the preferences, behaviors, and expectations of your new audience. This allows you to adapt visual and narrative elements while staying true to your brand's core.

Let's delve into a real-world example to illustrate this concept. Suppose I'm pitching to a hospitality client looking to appeal to a younger demographic without alienating their existing customer base:

"Hello Team,

I appreciate the opportunity to work with you. Our approach is rooted in maintaining the core values and essence of your esteemed brand—luxury, comfort, and exceptional service. We understand your aspiration to connect with a younger audience while preserving loyalty among your current patrons.

Our strategy involves a creative evolution that respects your brand's heritage while injecting modernity and relevance. We propose a visually dynamic campaign that incorporates vibrant, Instagram-worthy visuals and user-generated content to appeal to millennials and Gen Z.

Through personalized messaging and influencer partnerships, we aim to amplify your brand's reach across digital platforms while maintaining the high standards of service that your clientele expects.

Our past successes with similar luxury brands have resulted in significant increases in social engagement and direct bookings. We look forward to collaborating closely with your team to achieve similar success, tailored specifically to your unique market positioning."

This pitch illustrates how to respect brand consistency while creatively evolving to meet new objectives and target audience preferences. It emphasizes measurable outcomes and a tailored approach that aligns with both the client's goals and market trends. By balancing tradition and innovation, you can ensure your brand remains relevant and resonant across diverse demographics.

BRAND EVOLUTION AND MARKET PITCH ROADMAP

As we've discussed the importance of balancing brand consistency with creative adaptation, let's explore a structured approach—designing a roadmap for evolving your brand and effectively pitching to new markets and clients. This journey begins with solid groundwork and strategic adjustments tailored to insights from new audiences.

SCOUT THE COMPETITION

Kick things off by figuring out who your main rivals are in the new playground. Take a good look at what they're nailing and where they're not quite hitting the mark. This is your golden ticket to spot those juicy opportunities where you can really stand out. Say, for example, your competitors are wizards in digital ads but don't really get the whole community vibes thing – that's your chance to jump in and make a splash in that space.

Adapt Your Brand Story

When you're stepping into a new market, it's like blending into a new cultural party. You've got to tweak your brand's story so it feels right at home, without washing away what makes it uniquely yours. Consider it like tweaking your chat style and messages to mesh with local tastes—like telling jokes that everyone in the room understands.

Why not jazz up your content by mixing in some local slang, tossing in fun cultural facts, and sprinkling in some stats that locals will get? This way, your campaigns will really hit home, ramp up engagement, and send those conversion rates through the roof.

Customize Your Client Pitch

Get to know your new market by creating detailed client personas. Dive into what challenges they face, what motivates them, and how they behave. This knowledge helps you tailor your marketing strategies so they really resonate with each segment of your audience. When it comes to reaching out to potential clients, personalize those pitches. Show them exactly how your services can tackle their unique problems and boost their business. Say you're pitching to a retailer - you'd want to highlight how your digital marketing strategies can help get more people through the door and bump up their local online sales.

Digital Trends on Tap

Start chatting with potential clients right away using chatbots and AI tools. It's like having a real-time conversation, which can really make your customers' day and help build a stronger bond with them. Plus, it makes your brand come across as more friendly and on the ball.

When it comes to your campaigns, get personal. Craft your emails, ads, and social posts so they vibe with what your audience likes and does. It's like picking out a gift that's perfect for a friend. This approach gets people more excited about what you're saying and makes them feel like you're really talking to them, not just sending out generic blasts.

Localizing Your Digital Footprint

Start by giving your online presence a personal touch. If you want your website to really connect, use local SEO tricks and make sure your content really speaks the local biz lingo, hitting the spot for what the industry needs. On social media, hang out where your new market does and team up with influencers who get your new crowd. This can help you in building a bond that feels both familiar and exciting.

Showcase of Adaptability

Showing off how adaptable and skilled you are with some cool case studies from different sectors, especially ones that match up with the industry you're eyeing next, is a great way to show you're a jack-of-all-trades and can nail results in all sorts of situations. Plus, get in on the conversation by sharing your thoughts and publishing stuff that digs into the specific challenges and trends of the industry. You want to come across as that go-to, reliable buddy everyone wants to work with.

Metrics that Matter

When you dive into a new market or industry, pick out some key performance indicators (KPIs) to keep an eye on. Think about tracking stuff like how engaged people are, how often they're converting, and how happy your clients seem to be. This way, you can really get the gist of whether your strategies are hitting the mark. By constantly checking in on these numbers, you have the freedom to tweak and adjust your game plan. This keeps your agency nimble and on point, ready to take on whatever the market throws your way.

When you roll with these strategies, your digital marketing agency makes waves, paving the way for ongoing growth and success. Keep in mind, every new market is your chance to fine-tune your brand and show off how adaptable and skilled your agency is.

As we've journeyed through this exploration, it's clear that being adaptable is key for your brand as it grows. Remember, it is not just about your brand identity; it's about your whole agency. The digital marketing world is always on the move, always switching things up, so you've gotta stay on your toes and keep evolving. Keep that go-getter spirit alive as you dive into the exciting challenges coming your way.

CHAPTER 4

ASSEMBLING THE A-TEAM

Have you ever pondered what truly powers a successful digital marketing agency?

It's the team behind the scenes that makes everything possible. Zig Ziglar hit the nail on the head when he said, "You don't build a business; you build people, and then people build the business."

This idea shapes how we think about assembling our teams. Assembling our digital marketing agency's team is like putting together the Avengers—each hero brings unique strengths that, when combined, make our agency unstoppable. Who hasn't dreamt of assembling a team like the Avengers?

Think about it: You need a leader with vision, just like Captain America. Someone who can steer the team and keep everyone focused on the mission. Then there's the tech genius, your Thor, wielding the latest tools and innovations to smash through challenges. And the Black Widow of strategy, agile and sharp, is always a step ahead of the competition. Building an A-team means scouting for these superheroes and creating an "Agency Justice League" where diversity in skill sets and backgrounds saves the digital day.

Alright, strap in and let's explore how to gather your personal superhero squad, making sure your agency blasts right past its targets.

Let's kick things off by pinpointing the key players and the essential traits they bring to the table. This is about crafting a strong team ready to face whatever the digital space has in store.

FINDING THE RIGHT FIT FOR YOUR AGENCY

Think about the last time you tasted a dish that blew your mind. It likely had a special ingredient, something that stood out, yet perfectly complemented the rest. That's how critical it is to find the right people for your digital marketing agency. Every role is unique, and the right person doesn't just fill that role—they elevate it.

Leadership Pillars

Let's start by talking about the core pillars of leadership—the qualities that truly hold things together. Imagine someone not just moving forward but taking big leaps ahead. The first pillar is **vision**. Great leaders are the ones who see beyond the obvious, carving out new paths where others might see none. They're the trailblazers, creating a roadmap as they go and pushing the entire team toward bigger and better things.

Then there's **communication**, another crucial pillar. The best leaders know that motivating a team isn't just about tasks and targets—it's about sharing the right stories. Whether it's celebrating victories or reflecting on lessons learned, these leaders are masters at keeping their team inspired. They give feedback that's both motivating and insightful, making sure every team member feels connected to something bigger than just their daily to-do list.

And of course, there's **decisiveness**. This pillar is what keeps everything moving smoothly, especially when the waters get rough. Think of the leader as a captain steering the ship. Whether the seas are calm or stormy, they make quick, confident decisions that keep everyone on course. They know their team inside out, delegating wisely to ensure each person is in a role that plays to their strengths and keeps the whole operation running like clockwork.

The Technocrats

Next, we have the real driving force behind your agency—the technocrats.These are the minds that master the complex world of SEO, PPC, and analytics, ensuring your strategies hit the bullseye every single time. They don't just handle the technical side of things; they live and breathe it.

For technocrats, analyzing data is like second nature. While others might see a jumble of numbers, they see patterns, insights, and opportunities. Their expertise is what turns chaos into clarity, driving your campaigns with laser-focused precision. When challenges arise, they don't just find quick fixes—they deliver innovative solutions that push the boundaries of what's possible.

What sets these technocrats apart is their meticulous attention to detail. No stone is left unturned, no number unchecked, because excellence is the standard they live by.

Whether it's ensuring every pixel is in place or every keyword is optimized, their commitment to perfection ensures your campaigns run seamlessly.

But what truly keeps your agency ahead of the curve? It's their insatiable hunger for knowledge. As the digital world constantly evolves, technocrats are the first to dive into the latest tools, techniques, and trends.

Now, let's move into the essential qualities that truly make your team members stand out, regardless of their specific roles:

The Common Ground

Adaptability is key in digital marketing, just like it's essential in any fast-changing field. The best team members are those who can pivot quickly, embracing new tools and strategies as easily as they tackle unforeseen challenges. They lead the charge, ensuring your agency stays relevant and effective.

Collaboration is just as crucial. It doesn't matter if someone is leading your team or coding behind the scenes; the ability to work well with others amplifies their impact. These are the team players who boost everyone's performance by sharing ideas, providing support, and working together to solve problems. This synergy involves elevating every project and campaign you undertake.

Creativity also plays a key role. It's the spark that transforms a standard campaign into something memorable. Those who bring creative insights to the table don't just follow trends—they set them, turning each campaign into a showcase of innovation that captivates your audience.

Above all, being proactive is a game-changer. During interviews, it's crucial to look beyond technical skills and experience. Ask about times they anticipated challenges or seized opportunities without waiting for direction. Their answers can reveal a lot about their ability to drive your agency forward. This proactive approach helps in preventing problems, keeping your projects smooth, and your clients happy.

Before we dive deep into the art of nailing interviews, let me peel back the curtain on my own journey of building a team. In the early days of my agency, filling skill gaps was my top priority - tasks I couldn't handle alone, which at that time included design and SEO.I applied a simple economic principle: with a steady flow of high-paying branding projects, I decided to bring on board a designer who was slightly above my paygrade, and an SEO expert who fit snugly within my budget.

That was a learning experience. The designer, though talented, was a know-it-all, delaying tasks and being difficult to work with. Despite running the agency, I constantly felt belittled by the designer. This person habitually delayed tasks until the last minute, showed no willingness to accommodate, and dictated pricing and process-related work, essentially branding me a novice directly to my face. On the other hand, the SEO person, someone many of you who know Digital Ozone will recognize, turned out to be a gem. Despite having limited skills initially, he was eager to learn and constantly upgraded himself. He became an integral part of the team, contributing to technical discussions, building teams, and growing with the agency.

This experience taught me a valuable lesson about hiring. While it's essential to fill skills gaps, it's equally important to hire people who are eager to grow and align with your vision. The stage of your agency matters too. In the startup phase, you can focus more on intent and potential. As you scale, you need a mix of both intent and skill. Finding the right balance is crucial for building a team that grows with your agency.

THE TENNER TRACK

When it comes to hiring the right people for your team, the Tenner Track is a tool I've developed to make sure we find not just good candidates, but the perfect fit. It goes beyond the usual checklist of qualifications and experience. Instead of getting caught up in resumes that all start to look the same, the Tenner Track digs deeper, helping you discover the qualities that make someone a real asset to your agency.

Think of it as a roadmap for identifying those candidates who won't just get the job done, but who will thrive in your culture and push your team forward. It helps you zero in on the intangible qualities that don't always show up on paper. These are the traits that will make a difference when challenges arise and innovation is needed.

#1 The Icebreaker

Think of the start of each interview as the warm-up before the main event. I often begin with an icebreaker that's simple yet revealing. For instance, you might ask, "What's the most engaging project you've ever worked on, and what did you love about it?" This question does more than just break the ice; it offers a window into what drives the candidate, showcasing their enthusiasm and hinting at whether they'll mesh with the energetic pace of your team.

#2 Team Dynamics Decoder

Moving beyond the icebreaker, it's essential to gauge how a candidate collaborates within a team. After all, effective digital marketing is built on seamless teamwork. You could follow up with, "Could you tell me about a time you had to collaborate closely with a team? What was your role, and how did you contribute to achieving a common goal?" This inquiry helps you understand their ability to integrate, interact, and potentially lead within a group setting. It's about finding someone who elevates the entire team's efforts.

#3 Culture Compatibility Check

The next critical question to ask is, "What kind of work environment do you thrive in?" This isn't just small talk—it's a strategic probe into whether they'll blend well with the atmosphere and pace of your agency. Each person's response can illuminate whether they prefer a structured, quiet setting or a dynamic, collaborative workspace. Their answer helps you gauge if they'll sync with the vibe at your agency, whether it's fast-paced and ever-evolving or more methodical and steady.

#4 The Missing Piece to the Puzzle

To understand how a new hire might enhance your team's capabilities, consider asking, "Our team excels at X and Y. How would your skills in Z complement and enhance our existing strengths?" This question does double duty. It shows you how aware they are of their own skills, how they envision integrating and elevating the group's dynamics. It's all about finding that missing piece—someone who can fill the gaps, bring in fresh perspectives, and ultimately push the entire team's boundaries to new heights.

#5 Cool Under Pressure

A great way to see if a candidate can handle stress and think on their feet is to throw a hypothetical challenge their way. You might ask, "Imagine you're given a project with tight deadlines and limited resources. How would you approach it?" This question is an opportunity to observe their thought process. How they tackle this scenario can tell you a lot about their ability to manage pressure, innovate under constraints, and prioritize tasks. Their response will provide insight into whether they can maintain composure and clarity when the going gets tough, a crucial trait for the fast-paced demands of agency life.

#6 Values Check

It's essential to determine how well a candidate's values sync with those of your agency. Asking something like, "Which of our agency's core values resonates most with you, and why?" helps gauge their personal and professional ethos. This question goes beyond checking if they've researched your company; it probes deeper into how their beliefs and values align with your culture. Their answers can shed light on their potential fit within your team, indicating how they might enrich your agency's environment.

#7 The Growth Mindset

As you delve into thee skills and values, a great question to ask is, "What's one skill you're currently working on improving, and why?" This opens up a conversation about their drive for self-improvement and highlights their growth mindset. It's revealing to hear how candidates identify their own areas for growth and the actions they're taking to advance. This shows their potential to evolve with the demands of your agency and their long-term value as they grow their capabilities.

THE TENNER TRACK
You are hired
Thank you
Hire the Right people!
1 The Ice breaker
2 Team Dynamics Decoder
3 Culture Compatability check
4 The missing piece to the puzzle
5 Cool under Pressure
6 Values Check
7 The Growth mindset
8 Behind the desk-The personal side
9 Feedback Fluency

#8 Behind the Desk- The Personal Side

Then, shifting the focus slightly, it's insightful to learn about what they do outside the office. Asking, "What's your go-to activity to unwind after a busy day at work?" gives you a peek into their personal life. This question helps you see how they balance stress and relaxation, and it can be a fun way to gauge whether their personality will gel well with the rest of your team. Knowing what recharges them can also hint at how they maintain energy and enthusiasm for work. These softer insights can be just as critical as professional skills in building a harmonious team that thrives both during and outside of work hours.

#9 Feedback Fluency

Focusing on a candidate's personal and professional growth, it is important to understand how candidates handle feedback, a revealing question to ask is, "Tell me about a time you received constructive criticism. How did you handle it?" This inquiry helps gauge their receptiveness and resilience. You're not just looking for someone who can accept feedback but someone who can use it as a stepping stone for personal and professional development. Their response will tell you a lot about their maturity and their potential to contribute positively to the team environment.

#10 Ready to Stretch?

Next, to understand their adaptability, consider asking, "If we were to take on a project that's outside your comfort zone, how would you tackle it?" This scenario-based question is key to identifying their ability to handle new challenges and their willingness to embrace them. It's important to see how they think on their feet and whether they view such situations as opportunities for growth or as hurdles.

BALANCING ACT

Following the tenner track we've keenly pursued, we've identified the superheroes your digital marketing agency needs. With these exceptional talents now part of your team, the next crucial step is cultivating an environment of empowerment and strong leadership. This will enable our superheroes to further harness their powers and flourish.

This concept was put to the test during the COVID-19 pandemic, a time that tested the mettle of many businesses. When we were forced to shut our office doors practically overnight, I made the swift decision to let our team take home all necessary systems and equipment. We went a step further by extending additional allowances and support to ensure everyone could work comfortably from their homes.

This period was tough, especially as we saw an immediate drop in clients from sectors like real estate and F&B. However, the trust and autonomy we placed in our team paid off remarkably. Our team members rallied, bringing their creativity and resilience to the fore. Within a month, not only did we stabilize, but our revenue grew by 120per cent as we successfully pivoted to take on multiple e-commerce and tech-related projects.

This experience underscored a powerful lesson: showing trust in your team encourages them to trust you back. It also highlighted how a culture of empowerment can lead to rapid adaptation and innovation, even during crises. By ensuring strong leadership and giving your team the autonomy to make decisions, you enable them to turn challenges into opportunities for growth.

CREATING LEADERS AT HOME

Let's explore how we can empower our teams and cultivate strong leadership within agencies

Weekly Huddle Hub

Start by creating an environment where communication flows openly. To facilitate this, regular team meetings are crucial.One effective way to do this is through regular "Weekly Huddle" sessions. In our agency, we have instituted what we call the "Weekly Huddle." During these sessions, the team gathers to discuss ongoing projects, share updates, and brainstorm solutions. This consistent practice keeps everyone connected, involved, and aligned with the agency's goals.

Letting Leaders Rise

Empowerment grows when team members are given the chance to lead. By assigning project ownership, you're ensuring accountability and encouraging people to step up. When they're trusted to take charge, team members naturally grow into leadership roles and start driving projects with more initiative.

GROWTH MODE

When your team grows, so does your agency. Personalized development plans, whether through mastering new software or attending industry conferences, keep your team sharp and innovative. These investments come back tenfold when someone brings a fresh idea or tool that sets your agency apart.

Cheers to You

Recognizing effort really boosts motivation. Whether it's a "Team Member of the Month" program or a thoughtful reward like concert tickets for someone who loves music, showing appreciation in a meaningful way helps keep your team engaged and loyal. Cheering them on makes all the difference!

Flexibility that Fuels Success

Promoting work-life balance is absolutely essential in today's fast-paced world. By offering flexible hours, remote work options, and wellness initiatives such as yoga and mindfulness sessions, we can effectively manage stress and ignite creativity.

When team members feel supported and valued, they're also more engaged and productive.

When you put these practices and policies to work, you're setting up a winning culture. It's all about boosting leadership, strengthening team connections, and pushing your agency to achieve even more success.

GLOBAL GALLERY

Ogilvy's Commitment to Diversity and Cultivating Talent

To truly grasp the benefits of diverse teams in digital marketing agencies, let's take a journey around the world and see how these dynamics unfold on a global stage.

Ogilvy, a powerhouse in the global marketing scene, really sets the standard when it comes to embracing diversity, equity, and inclusion (DE&I). Their commitment is a big part of what makes their teams so robust, innovative, and successful.

Ogilvy's DE&I Initiatives: "The Force Innovation Lab"

In 2021, Ogilvy didn't just talk the talk; they walked it with the launch of "The Force," a diversity innovation lab. This isn't your typical committee meeting. Imagine a think tank where creative minds from across industries converge to solve DE&I challenges using behavioral science and design thinking. They're tackling everything from developing talent pipelines to improving funding and staffing—all in the name of integrating DE&I into the fabric of business strategies. It's about collaboration, not competition, and it's changing the game.

Empowering Leadership and Nurturing Talent Then there's Ogilvy's "30 for 30" leadership program, specifically uplifting women across its global offices. This isn't just another leadership seminar; it's a career accelerator combining group projects, deep reflection, and real empowerment. The results? More promotions, higher retention, and a flood of opportunities. And let's not overlook how Ogilvy onboards its interns and graduates. They're grooming the next gen of marketers with real chances to grow, thanks to solid partnerships with educational powerhouses.

Cultivating an Inclusive Workplace Ogilvy also puts its policies where its promises are. Think annual pay equity reviews, comprehensive unconscious bias training, and forums for open communication. Everyone's voice matters, and they make sure all voices are heard. It's about building a culture where everyone feels they belong, supported by regular check-ins to fine-tune their approach.

Let's dive deeper into how Ogilvy's embrace of diversity translates into tangible benefits for their team dynamics and creative output. Diversity at Ogilvy is the engine driving their creativity. When team members from varied backgrounds throw their ideas into the mix, the result is often unexpectedly brilliant. It's the kind of innovation you get when different perspectives challenge the norm, sparking solutions that would be unimaginable in a homogenous setting.

Handling disagreements is another area where Ogilvy shines. Their strategy is to equip everyone with conflict resolution skills and foster an atmosphere where diverse viewpoints are not just heard but respected. This transforms them into collaborative opportunities, strengthening team bonds and boosting overall morale.

And it's not all about resolving conflicts. Ogilvy's inclusive vibe significantly uplifts employee morale and keeps them around longer. Imagine working in a place where your's celebrated and where cultural events like Ramadan and Women's Day are embraced enthusiastically. It's the kind of supportive environment that makes employees feel at home, enhancing their commitment and driving them to give their best.

Ogilvy led the charge. By really embedding diversity into their core, they're always evolving and showing everyone what being truly inclusive looks like.

THE DIVERSE AGENCY

With a strong culture of empowerment and leadership in place, it's time to focus on another vital aspect: diversity and inclusion. By embracing diverse perspectives, you'll enhance the culture you've already built, making it richer and more dynamic.

True diversity values talent and individuality. At our agency, we create roles open to everyone, regardless of gender, age, abilities, or sexuality. This inclusivity fosters a workplace where everyone can thrive, enhancing our collective creativity and problem-solving skills.

To keep these efforts meaningful, we maintain open communication. Regular feedback and surveys help us gauge how well our initiatives are working, ensuring that everyone feels heard and valued. Celebrating cultural diversity through events and sharing personal stories strengthens team bonds and fosters a deeper sense of understanding.

By embedding diversity and inclusion into your agency, you create a space where all voices are valued. This approach boosts employee satisfaction, creativity, and innovation. A diverse team brings fresh perspectives, helping your agency connect with a wider range of clients and craft more resonant messages. This synergy will set your agency apart, fueling both growth and reputation.

WHERE THERE'S A BAND, THERE WILL BE SOME MUSIC

In a diverse team, just like in a band, you can expect different notes to collide at times. Conflicts are a natural part of any collaborative environment, but if handled right, they can create harmony rather than chaos. Think of conflict resolution as tuning the instruments so the music flows smoothly.

Aim for Harmony

When conflict arises, it's not just about reaching the end goal—it's about finding a way to work together harmoniously. Encourage your team to stay outcome-driven by framing the conversation around solutions rather than dwelling on the issue itself. For example, when a recent project at our agency hit a snag, we shifted our focus from the disagreement to the solution. By realigning everyone's attention to the desired result, we were able to tackle the challenges and come out stronger.

A Symphony of Support

Creating a supportive environment is like crafting a perfect acoustics room. It enhances each note's clarity and richness. By creating a setting where everyone feels valued, conflicts are less frequent and more manageable. This supportive backdrop makes it easier for team members to approach disagreements with a collaborative rather than confrontational attitude.

EMPATHY: THE HEART OF RESOLUTION

Empathy is like understanding the soul of the music. When conflicts arise, stepping into your colleagues' shoes to understand their perspective can transform discord into constructive collaboration. This was evident when a project hiccup felt overwhelming to a team member; showing empathy and support turned the situation from a solo struggle into a duet of problem-solving.

TURNING DISSONANCE INTO HARMONY

Every conflict offers a chance to fine-tune our team's dynamics. By promoting a culture where compromise and collaboration are the norms, we ensure that each challenge leads to stronger unity and better solutions. As we wrap up this discussion on the human aspects of your agency, you now have a deeper understanding of how to nurture a team that's talented, harmonious and resilient. With these tools in hand, you're ready to tackle the next crucial steps: fine-tuning the operational side of things. Let's move forward together, smoothing out the rough edges and shaping an agency that's as efficient as it is innovative.

CHAPTER 5

MATCHMAKING MASTERY

Let's be honest: no matter how perfectly you've assembled your A-team, what truly makes a difference in your digital marketing agency is your ability to build and nurture client relationships. It's funny how this essential part of your business can sometimes feel like a marriage, complete with vows to deliver success and the occasional need for couple's therapy sessions when expectations clash.

In the domain of digital marketing, this relationship dynamic is no laughing matter. The bond you forge with your clients can determine the longevity of your agency itself. Fostering strong, respectful partnerships with your clients isn't just about keeping them happy in the short term; it's about creating lasting bonds that turn one-off projects into ongoing collaborations. Let's explore the subtle art of aligning client expectations and nurturing these relationships to ensure they grow stronger over time.

What do you think lies at the heart of forging successful relationships with your clients? If you guessed aligning their expectations with your agency's deliverables, you're right on target.Given the complex nature of our industry, where campaigns evolve and strategies shift, starting on the same page is crucial. This alignment involves setting the stage for all the benefits that come with a clear understanding between you and your client.

WHY IT'S ESSENTIAL

First, think about the increase in client satisfaction and retention. When clients have a clear understanding of what to expect from you and you consistently deliver on those promises, satisfaction will naturally follow. A satisfied client is a loyal one, likely to return and possibly recommend your outstanding service to others.

Then there's scope creep—the bane of many projects. Without clear boundaries, projects can grow wildly beyond their initial outlines, straining budgets and timelines. By setting definitive deliverables and expectations right from the start, both parties understand the scope, reducing the risk of last-minute surprises or unplanned expansions.

Building trust is another critical outcome. In digital marketing, where results can sometimes take time to manifest, being seen as trustworthy can make or break your agency. Meet or exceed the expectations you've set, and you cement your agency's credibility, making it easier to win new projects and referrals.

CRAFTING THE INITIAL PROPOSAL

Even in the early days when your pitch might not be bulletproof or your service offerings fully polished, clarity and justification in your proposals are crucial. For many digital marketing agencies, the beginning is about setting clear, understandable expectations—almost like building a foundation stone by stone. What always resonated with my clients was a transparent, piecemeal approach to our proposals. By breaking down services and costs clearly, we sanitized our basic service structure and pricing, gradually building trust. This method allows clients to start small, and as their confidence in our capabilities grows, so does their commitment to our services.

As we move forward, think of aligning expectations with a technique I like to call **"Planning a 5-Course Meal."** This isn't really about food, but rather about carefully planning every step of how you engage with your clients.

COOKING UP A CLEAR PROJECT SCOPE

Just like a well-planned recipe, a detailed project scope document is your guide to success. This document lays out everything from appetizers to desserts: the deliverables, the timelines, the milestones, and the roles each party plays. It's crucial to be clear about what is included and, just as importantly, what isn't. This clarity prevents future misunderstandings and sets a professional tone. It reassures your client that your agency handles its projects with precision and attention to detail.

GETTING TO KNOW YOUR DINERS

How well do you really know your client's taste? Just as a chef interviews guests about dietary preferences, conducting detailed client questionnaires or discovery sessions before the project starts is key. These interactions help you uncover your client's business objectives, brand voice, and target audience. They allow you to tailor your strategies and proposals precisely to their needs. More than just gathering information, these sessions show your clients that their specific goals are your priority, and you're committed to customizing your services to align perfectly with their expectations.

CHEF'S SPECIALS

Consider that you're deciding whether to try a new restaurant. What's one of the first things you do? Likely, you check the reviews and photos of their specials. Similarly, sharing compelling case studies and testimonials from satisfied clients works wonders. This part of our meal showcases your agency's ability to whip up impressive results, serving as tangible proof of your expertise. When clients see the successful campaigns you've crafted for others, particularly those in similar industries, their confidence in your abilities grows. It's about showing, not just telling, that you can deliver on your promises.

THE ART OF TABLE SERVICE

No matter how delicious a meal is, it can be ruined by poor service. The same goes for client relationships. Establishing open lines of communication is like ensuring your waitstaff is attentive and responsive. Setting up clear protocols for how and when you'll provide updates, who the client can reach out to with questions, and how you'll handle any issues that arise, is crucial. These protocols ensure that the client feels valued and informed every step of the way, fostering a relationship built on trust and mutual respect.

NO OVERPROMISING

One of the most essential ingredients in any partnership is transparency. It's crucial to be upfront about what your agency can realistically deliver within the agreed timeline and budget. Rather than embellishing capabilities or promising the moon, focus on what's achievable. Lay out a clear roadmap of the steps your team will take to meet these goals, ensuring that expectations are aligned from the outset. This approach reduces the risk of misunderstandings and builds a foundation of trust.

Lay out a clear roadmap
to your team on what's
ACHIEVABLE !!

As you wrap up your proposal, it's important to discuss financials with a strategy that benefits both parties. Avoid the temptation to undercut your own value with excessive discounts or freebies, which can devalue your services. Instead, consider offering staged proposals, especially beneficial for clients who are new to digital marketing or those who have had less than stellar experiences in the past. Start with a smaller package at a lower rate, allowing them to experience the value you provide. As their confidence in your capabilities grows, you can introduce more comprehensive packages. Remember, while offering initial lower rates can open doors, setting clear timelines and deliverables is essential to ensure you're not compromising your margins permanently.

FROM ALIGNMENT TO ACTION: THE ONBOARDING EXPERIENCE

After aligning client expectations with your deliverables, what comes next? The answer here lies in action, particularly through a robust onboarding process. This phase is far from just another item on the checklist. It's the moment where you begin to translate theoretical plans into concrete actions. Think of onboarding as the first chapter in your client relationship story. This is where you transform promises into actions. The way you handle onboarding can significantly influence how your client perceives your competence and commitment. A smooth and impressive onboarding experience reassures your client of their choice and builds excitement and trust, establishing a positive tone for all future interactions.

The transition from signing the contract to initiating services should be seamless. This phase is your opportunity to showcase your agency's organizational skills and attention to detail. By efficiently setting up processes, communicating clearly, and making the necessary introductions, you demonstrate professionalism and dedication—qualities that reassure clients they're in capable hands.

Never underestimate the power of a good first impression. Onboarding is your chance to reinforce the client's decision to work with you.

When it comes to onboarding, blending a well-structured process with a personal touch isn't just helpful—it's essential.

Especially for new agency founders, where personal branding and prior experience play pivotal roles in securing clients, being actively involved in the early phases of client interaction is crucial.

I recommend adopting a 'no-excuse show-up clause' during the first three months for your initial 10 clients. This commitment ensures you are present for every strategy call and meeting, allowing you to refine your onboarding process based on direct feedback and first-hand experiences. Remember, these first interactions are about setting your agency's standard.

Digital marketing is not a quick fix but a strategic endeavor that shows its real value over time. For any digital service, a period of three months is a reasonable timeframe to establish processes, implement strategies, and begin seeing tangible results. Make this clear to your clients upfront to set realistic expectations and prevent premature judgments about the effectiveness of your strategies.

FRAMEWORK FOR SEAMLESS ONBOARDING

To start every client relationship off on the right note, it's super important to have a solid onboarding plan in place. Here's a tried-and-true framework that'll help make the onboarding process seamless. Remember, it's not just about checking off tasks; it's about setting the stage for a winning partnership.

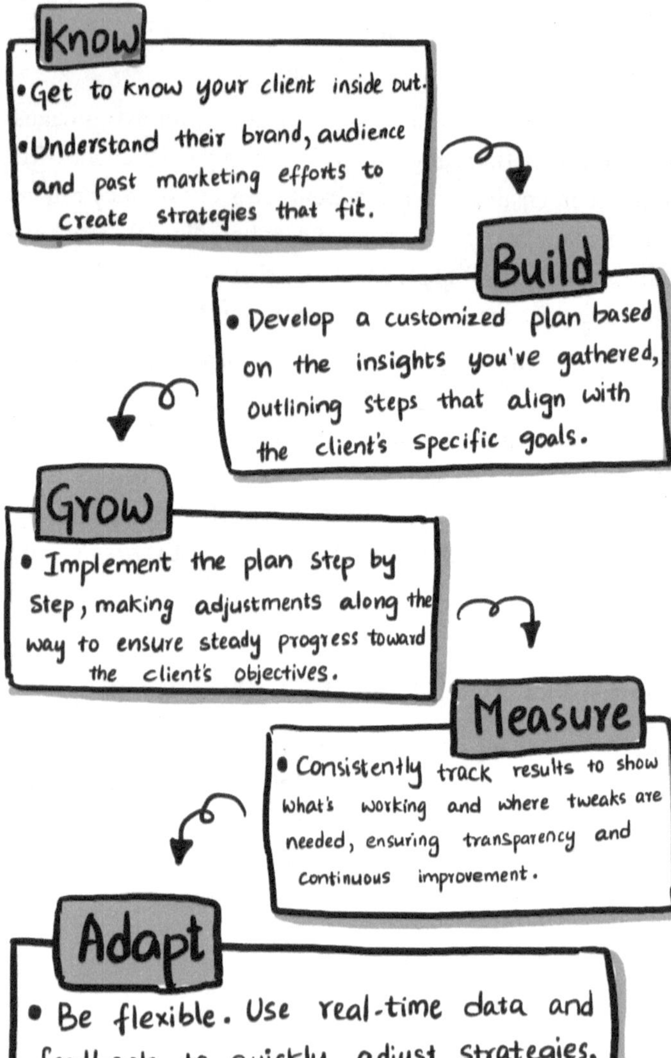
Know
• Get to know your client inside out.
• Understand their brand, audience and past marketing efforts to create strategies that fit.
Build
• Develop a customized plan based on the insights you've gathered, outlining steps that align with the client's specific goals.
Grow
• Implement the plan step by step, making adjustments along the way to ensure steady progress toward the client's objectives.
Measure
• Consistently track results to show what's working and where tweaks are needed, ensuring transparency and continuous improvement.
Adapt
• Be flexible. Use real-time data and feedback to quickly adjust strategies, staying ahead of market shifts & client needs.

UNIFYING LANGUAGE AND PROCESSES

Create a roadmap for onboarding, starting with a detailed client onboarding form that keeps everyone on your team aligned. This way, it doesn't matter if a client is chatting with a strategist, a designer, or even the founder - they get the same awesome level of info and service. Going this route cuts down on the confusion and really boosts your clients' confidence in what your agency can do.

By really sticking to this framework, you're setting up an onboarding experience that wows new clients and builds a solid base for their long-term success and growth. Let me reiterate the key idea here: Make clients feel right off the bat that choosing you was the best decision they've made.

THE RAINBOW EFFECT

Now that you've seamlessly gotten through the onboarding rapids with finesse, what's next? How do you ensure that this isn't just a honeymoon phase with your clients? This is where the real work begins to foster longevity in your client relationships.

Sustaining a lively and evolving relationship with clients is a must-have. It's what keeps your agency smack in the middle of your clients' success stories, always ready to adapt to their needs and the constantly shifting market. So, how do you keep this relationship alive and thriving?

Welcome to what I like to call the Rainbow Effect. It's about bringing color into the relationship after the initial storm—where the storm is the flurry of setup and onboarding, and the rainbow symbolizes the ongoing engagement that leads to a treasure trove of mutual benefits. This idea entails proving you're an essential partner your clients can't do without.

THE RAINBOW EFFECT
- Bring color into the relationship
Red
Empathy
Orange
Sincere effort
Yellow
Honest reporting
Wins
Challenges
Green
Always learning attitude
Blue
Respect for Expertise
Indigo
Setting Boundaries
Violet
Reboot, Renew, Review
R

Lets now dive into the "colors" of this rainbow, each representing a crucial aspect of long-term client relationships.

Empathy (Red)

Empathy connects you with clients on a human level. Understanding their emotional needs builds trust, especially during tough times. For example, when a client's struggling with a brand refresh, acknowledging their stress and adapting your approach strengthens the partnership.

Sincere Effort (Orange)

Going the extra mile shows commitment. Suggesting creative ideas or additional research for a client's product launch signals your dedication to their success. It's about showing you're invested in their win, not just completing a task.

Honest Reporting (Yellow)

Transparency fosters trust. Candid updates about both wins and challenges give clients a clear picture. Providing actionable insights based on analytics shows integrity and keeps clients engaged in shaping the campaign's direction.

Always Learning Attitude (Green)

Digital marketing evolves quickly, and your agency must stay ahead. Continuously embracing new tools and trends ensures innovation. For example, adapting to new algorithm changes keeps your clients' campaigns cutting-edge and effective.

Respect for Expertise (Blue)

Specialized knowledge drives success. When a client needs a top-tier e-commerce strategy, having an expert in-house boosts the campaign's impact. Valuing expertise shows clients you're serious about delivering the best results.

Setting Boundaries (Indigo)

Clear boundaries safeguard creativity and focus. Establishing defined hours for client calls keeps your team energized while maintaining client satisfaction. This approach prevents burnout and ensures consistent quality in every project.

Reboot, Renew, and Review (Violet)

Refresh strategies (Reboot) by embracing new trends, celebrate milestones (Renew) during client anniversaries, and hold regular assessments (Review) to keep campaigns on track. These steps reinforce the value of your agency and build long-term relationships.

Integrating these principles into your client engagement strategy helps your agency keep a close eye on how healthy your client relationships are, while also pushing them forward. Taking this proactive approach makes sure your partnerships last and are good for both sides. It's all about the Rainbow Effect, where every color (or in this case, every client) plays a vital role.

GLOBAL GALLERY

R/GA and Nike: A Rainbow of Innovation in Client Relationships

Let's take a closer look at the global scene and check out an example that showcases the "Rainbow Effect" framework.— R/GA's long-standing partnership with Nike. This is a story of how bringing the right colors into your client relationships can create something truly lasting and impactful.

Empathy (Red): Tuning into Nike's Pulse

R/GA's success with Nike stems from deep empathy. By fully understanding Nike's brand and its audience, they create campaigns that truly resonate. When your agency taps into what drives your client, you forge stronger, more emotional connections that go beyond surface-level marketing.

Sincere Effort (Orange): Going the Extra Mile

R/GA's partnership with Nike thrives on sincere effort. Whether it's pioneering digital campaigns or pushing creative boundaries, their dedication is clear. This commitment transforms good collaborations into great ones, where both sides are fully invested in success.

Honest Reporting (Yellow): Transparency Builds Trust

R/GA's transparent communication strengthens trust with Nike. They provide honest results, even when things don't go as planned. This openness ensures Nike feels informed and involved, building a relationship based on mutual trust and clarity.

Always Learning Attitude (Green): Staying Ahead of the Curve

R/GA thrives on continuous learning, keeping Nike's campaigns fresh and relevant by staying ahead of trends. This commitment ensures their strategies are always forward-thinking, something every agency should embrace to stay competitive.

Respect for Expertise (Blue): Harnessing Specialized Knowledge

R/GA values expertise, backing innovative ideas with deep knowledge. By integrating specialized insights into Nike's campaigns, they create highly effective strategies, showing Nike they understand what it takes to execute top-notch campaigns.

Setting Boundaries (Indigo): Keeping Projects on Track

R/GA sets clear boundaries with Nike, respecting timelines and deliverables. This approach creates a structured, productive partnership where creativity thrives without the risk of scope creep or miscommunication.

Reboot, Renew, and Review (Violet): Keeping the Partnership Fresh

R/GA continually reevaluates strategies with Nike, keeping campaigns dynamic and forward-looking. This regular refresh ensures both the agency and client stay aligned and ready for future growth.

For any agency looking to build lasting, impactful relationships, R/GA's approach is a shining example of what's possible when you truly commit to bringing your best to the table, every single day.

As we unravel the aspects of the Rainbow Effect, detailing the spectrum of strategies that nurture long-term client relationships, it's important to recognize that not every day is sunlit. Sometimes, clouds gather, and disagreements or conflicts arise. How you deal with these storms can strengthen the bonds with your clients, turning potential setbacks into opportunities for growth.

CONFLICT IS INEVITABLE, BUT COMBAT IS OPTIONAL

Disagreements are bound to happen, even when everything seems perfectly aligned. In the fast-paced, subjective world of digital marketing, it's not about avoiding conflict but managing it with skill and professionalism. The goal is to handle these moments thoughtfully, ensuring they don't escalate into full-blown combat. Here, I would like to introduce an approach that will guide you through managing conflicts with a structured, thoughtful process that resolves issues and fortifies the relationship.

Coffee Cup Conundrum

Imagine this: You're sitting across from your client, a cup of coffee in hand, the aroma mingling in the air like the shared goal of resolving a thorny issue. This isn't just a casual chat; it's the first critical step in the "Embrace, Execute, Employ" strategy—where you embrace the conflict with openness and a willingness to understand.

The coffee cup scenario isn't just about enjoying a good brew; it's symbolic of the warmth and mutual respect needed to dissolve tensions. It's where you listen intently, not to respond, but to understand. Here, every sip is a moment to consider not just what went wrong, but how your client feels about it.

As you discuss, employ creativity as your ally. This isn't about finding a quick fix but crafting a solution that addresses the root of the issue. Engage in a brainstorming session right there, with napkins as notepads, sketching out ideas that can turn challenges into opportunities for growth.

The goal of this conversation is to leave a pleasant aftertaste; a resolution that both parties feel good about. It's about ensuring that by the time the coffee cups are empty, you've laid the groundwork for a solution that feels as satisfying as that last sip of coffee—rich, full-bodied, and exactly what was needed.

Jazz Jam Session

Now that you've embraced the conflict, it's time to jazz things up with the next phase: execution. Think of resolving conflicts like a jazz performance, where each unexpected note is not a mistake but an invitation to innovate. It's about making music, not discord.

In jazz, dissonance is often the launch pad for the most memorable parts of the performance. Similarly, in your client relationships, recognize that disagreements are not setbacks but opportunities to explore new ideas. Encourage a back-and-forth dialogue where you and your client can riff off each other's ideas creatively.

Just as jazz musicians do not stick rigidly to the sheet music, be flexible in how you approach solutions. This might mean adjusting your strategy mid-project or introducing new tools or methods that better align with the client's evolving needs. The key is to keep the communication open and fluid, allowing both sides to contribute to the final outcome.

The goal of this "session" is to reach a harmony that satisfies all involved parties. This means finding a rhythm in your interactions that feels good and productive. It's about blending your agency's expertise with the client's deep knowledge of their own business to compose a new melody—one that resonates with the client's goals and exceeds their expectations.

PIXEL PUZZLE APPROACH

Think of conflict resolution like solving a jigsaw puzzle where every piece is vital to the final picture. Each conflict and every small detail reveals crucial insights that help align your team and client towards a common goal.

It's about fine-tuning—adjusting strategies and improving communication to make sure everyone's on the same page. For instance, a project may hit a snag due to differing views on the timeline. Instead of pushing ahead with the original plan, taking a step back to realign on the schedule could turn a potential conflict into a productive discussion, enhancing collaboration.

The process culminates in what I call the 'Puzzle Completion Strategy,' where every piece—every resolved issue—adds to a coherent whole. Just like a well-assembled puzzle, this collective effort not only resolves conflicts but strengthens relationships, ensuring all parties are invested and satisfied with the outcome. This method not only resolves tensions but transforms them into opportunities for deeper understanding and cooperation.

In closing, I want to leave you with this thought: how will you ensure that every client feels valued and understood from the very first conversation to the final handover?The ideas we've covered aren't just strategies—they're a way to build real, lasting partnerships. Now it's your turn to put them into action and see the difference they can make in creating connections that are both meaningful and productive.

To leave you with a thought to carry forward in your journey, remember the words of Maya Angelou, who captured the essence of any relationship: ***"People will forget what you said, people will forget what you did, but people will never forget how you made them feel."*** This is particularly resonant in the context of client relationships. Each interaction is an opportunity to make a lasting impression, to create a feeling of trust and valued partnership that stands the test of time.

Collaboration can turn out a potential conflict into a productive discussion

CHAPTER 6

SHOW ME THE MONEY

In the world of digital marketing, where creative campaigns and viral trends often steal the spotlight, there's another star performer who doesn't quite get the glamorous headlines: Money. Yes, you heard it right. We're talking cold, hard cash and how it often seems to play hide and seek just when we need it most.

Numbers can be daunting, especially when you'd rather brainstorm the next viral campaign than pore over spreadsheets. But building a rock-solid financial foundation is as crucial as nailing that perfect logo design. It's what keeps the lights on and our creative juices flowing. As it is famously said, "A goal without a plan is just a wish." And when it comes to transforming your digital agency from a wishful thought to a towering reality, understanding the nitty-gritty of finances is non-negotiable.

MONEY MATTERS

Taking the leap from the world of creativity, where your biggest concern was matching Pantone shades or finessing that last-minute client request, to running the whole show is a bit like jumping from the frying pan into the fire. Suddenly, you're not just creating; you're calculating, strategizing, and, yes, tackling the big, bad world of finances.

If you are feeling overwhelmed, know that you're not alone. Every creative soul turned agency founder has been there—staring down the barrel of cash flow forecasts and investment decisions. But fear not because we're about to demystify this financial maze together.

The First Leap: Starting your own agency isn't just about having a killer portfolio; it's about pouring both your creative energy and some cash into making it happen. From getting your legal stuff sorted to setting up your digital presence (hello, website!), those early expenses can feel like a bit of a gamble. But let's be real—being your own boss comes with a price tag. Make sure you've got a safety net with at least six months of backup. So, if your monthly expense is 1 lakh, set aside 6 lakhs to stay steady as you launch.

Embracing the Numbers Game: Shifting from your creative groove to budgets and balance sheets might feel like entering unfamiliar territory. But here's the truth: you've got the skills to ace this. The same creative thinking you apply to crafting campaigns can help you plan your pricing and map out your finances. Start by defining clear pricing strategies that align with the value you deliver—whether it's hourly rates, project-based pricing, or retainers. Then, break down your expenses and set financial goals.

This isn't about getting lost in spreadsheets—it's about making the numbers work for you, so you can keep your business thriving. Set aside time to review your cash flow, plan for growth, and make sure you have a clear picture of what's coming in and going out.

The Ebb and Flow of Cash: Imagine you've just crafted the most epic campaign. The client loves it, you're on cloud nine, and then... you wait. And wait. Because while the accolades are instant, payments, my friend, are not. This cash flow conundrum is like being promised the best dessert after a meal, but it arrives only when you're about to leave the restaurant. Managing when money comes in and goes out is crucial, lest you find your agency's engine sputtering just when you need to speed up.

The Unexpected Expenses: Just when you think you've mastered your finances, unexpected expenses show up like uninvited guests at a party. Maybe it's your trusty laptop giving up the ghost mid-project, or suddenly realizing you need a new tool for a client's campaign yesterday. These unplanned expenses can sprint through your savings like they're trying to break a world record.

Here's where your contingency fund comes into play, acting as your agency's safety net. Setting aside a portion of your budget for unexpected costs ensures that surprise expenses won't throw you off track. While it might feel like you're pulling from immediate resources, this move safeguards your agency's future and keeps things running smoothly, even when those inevitable bumps arise.

THE PRICE IS RIGHT... OR IS IT?

Getting through the tricky waters of pricing is a bit like playing Goldilocks in the digital marketing world. Set your prices too low, and you risk becoming the bargain bin option, attracting clients who might not value your true worth. Price your services too high, and you could scare away potential business faster than swiping left on a mismatched Tinder profile.

It's about finding the balance between what you're worth and what the market will bear.

Every project you take on is an investment. Your time, creativity, and resources are limited, so when you accept a low-paying project, you're essentially using up those valuable assets on something that doesn't push you forward. On the flip side, pricing too high can shut doors to projects that could build long-term relationships or open up new opportunities. It's a balancing act, and getting it wrong can cost you more than just money—it can cost you growth.

30-20-50 PROFITABILITY MODEL

Pricing isn't a guessing game. A solid pricing strategy is non-negotiable. You need a plan that covers your costs and leaves room for growth, ensuring that each project contributes meaningfully to your long-term success. For me, the **30-20-50 Profitability Model** has been my go-to method, a thumb rule I swear by when deciding which projects to take on. It's a pricing strategy that provides a clear roadmap, guiding you to strike that crucial balance. A 5-10 percent deviation might be acceptable now and then, but anything beyond that puts you at risk of undercutting your potential growth or overextending yourself. This model has consistently kept me grounded, ensuring my business stays on a steady upward path.

By integrating this model into your pricing strategy, you're setting up a framework for sustained success, ensuring that every step—from landing new clients to scaling your services—keeps profitability at the core. It's about building your agency on a financial foundation that's solid and flexible enough to support both the early growth stages and long-term sustainability.

30-20-50 PROFITABILITY MODEL

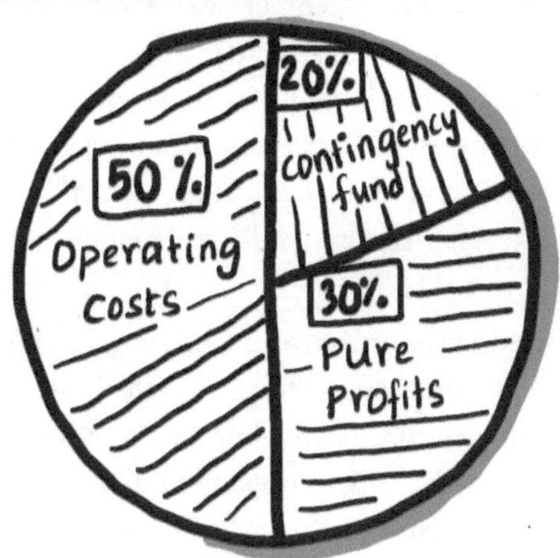

5-10% devation might be acceptable, but not beyond.

This model helps for long term success

under pricing

Over Pricing

Overpricing or underpricing disrupts growth

3 1 2

When I first launched my digital marketing agency, it was a leap driven by passion, but it needed structure to survive. Like crafting a strategy for a new campaign, I analyzed every aspect of the business—measuring potential profits against the costs. Hiring that first team member was a calculated risk, made possible because of a consistent income stream from service retainers. That's where the 30-20-50 Profitability Model came into play; setting aside 30 per cent as a pure profit, 20 per cent as contingency fund, and dedicating 50 per cent to ongoing expenses like salaries, rent, software/equipment or any other fixed cost.

As the agency grew, so did this model. What was once earmarked as contingency fund or safety nets began to be reinvested strategically, channeling funds into assets and tools that fueled growth. This reinvestment allowed me to take on larger projects, expand the team, and aim for long-term gains. Each decision, whether taking on new clients or making key hires, was rooted in this model, ensuring the agency's growth was sustainable and well-paced.

This approach was about smart allocations, from figuring out manpower needs to smoothing out plan appraisals and even renewing service agreements with a sharper lens. It's this kind of balanced thinking that helps you take on projects with confidence, knowing that every move is setting you up for bigger wins down the road.

SCALING FROM SOLO

Once you've laid down the foundation with a solid pricing strategy like the 30-20-50 model, you're paving the way for growth. With your finances balanced and the right structure in place, the next natural step is scaling. Scaling is the dream, but it comes with its own set of challenges. Hiring, expanding your services, maybe even upgrading from your home office to an actual one – all this needs more than just pocket change. It's about investing in your growth without stretching yourself too thin. This transition isn't just about throwing money at the situation. It's all about who you know. Seriously, networking is key –it's all about making those real, solid connections in the industry. These are the folks who can bring in new clients, the talented people itching to join your squad, and the partnerships that'll skyrocket your business.

Thinking about moving to a bigger space or adding some new services? Don't forget how crucial it is to mingle with others in your field. Hit up industry meetups, dive into online forums, and never underestimate the power of a good coffee chat. Pouring into these relationships is just as vital as any cash you're investing in your agency's growth. Your network is a goldmine that can seriously push your agency ahead. So, make sure you're giving those connections the TLC they deserve as you dream about scaling up.

THE FINANCIAL GROWTH TREE

As you scale your agency and look towards bigger goals, it's important to recognize that growth needs deep roots, much like a tree that offers both shade and fruit as it matures. This brings us to your financial growth tree—a structure that, when nurtured well, becomes the foundation of your growth, ensuring stability and sustainability. Picture your agency's financial plan as this very tree, with every aspect of your finances serving as a branch, each one essential to the health of the whole.

Much like any strong tree, the roots of your financial growth tree dig deep, keeping everything grounded as you continue to grow upward. These roots—your steady cash flow, clear pricing strategies like the 30-20-50 model, and a reserve for unexpected needs—ensure that your growth is stable, not rushed or haphazard. They provide the nourishment that keeps your financial tree healthy as it branches out.

Now, let's look at the key parts of this tree:

Branching Out with Clarity

Think of this as finding your way through foggy finances. A clear financial plan lights the way, helping you steer clear of pitfalls and allowing your tree to grow without unnecessary stress. When you know where each dollar is going, your tree is less likely to be battered by financial storms.

Fueling Growth like a Steady Trunk

Your tree's trunk supports everything, just like a well-planned financial strategy powers your agency's growth. This structure ensures that you expand at the right pace, without overextending your resources. The trunk keeps your operations balanced and helps you stay on course.

Smart Decision-Making Branches

With your financial tree, each branch represents smart decisions—whether it's a sharp turn towards a new opportunity or a brake before you hit an obstacle. Each branch grows from the wisdom your financial growth tree provides, guiding you through both opportunities and challenges with agility.

Creative Heart Beats in the Leaves

The leaves of your tree are the creative ideas and projects that bloom when your financial health is in check. They show how well-nurtured and thriving your agency is. With a steady flow of resources, your creative efforts flourish without the constant worry of budgets or cash flow holding you back.

Planting Seeds for Future Growth

And finally, your financial tree allows you to plant seeds for the future—whether that's expanding your team or exploring new digital territories. With a strong plan, you're laying down the groundwork for continued growth, making sure every move you make is supported by solid financial health.

This financial growth tree ensures that your agency is not just standing tall but is deeply rooted and capable of weathering whatever comes its way.

Now that we've unlocked how the 30-20-50 model sets you up for smart, agile growth, let's move into the golden rules that can elevate your agency even further—rules that made all the difference for me and will do the same for you.

SCALE SMARTER

As our agency began to scale, guided by the principles of our financial growth tree, it became evident that the initial 30-20-50 profitability model needed a facelift. This adjustment was a strategic step to support our expanding operations without compromising on financial health or organizational culture.

There can be minor adjustments in this framework from time to time. As we reached a new growth phase profitability margins tightened to a precise 20 to 25 percent allowing us to scale more effectively. For the time being we also cut down on our contingency fund to a mere 10 per cent.

This reallocation made it possible to direct a substantial sixty five to seventy percent towards fixed costs such as rent, utilities, and most importantly salaries. We also optimised the use of financial tools like overdraft facilities till we boarded the next set of retainer clients and climbed back into the 30-20-50 ratio.

Because let's face it, our team is the real MVP here, and keeping them happy and motivated is what keeps the engine running smoothly. You should never pull out the contingency or pure profit from your team's pocket.

Let's take a look at how this financial growth tree and the updated 30-20-50 model played out in real-life scenarios at my agency. For example, one of our key team members, let's call him Rohan, was managing four major accounts and approached me for a raise. The revised model was instrumental in this situation. By assessing his contribution through the lens of our financial structure, we were able to make a fair and balanced decision. It recognized his value to the agency while ensuring we stayed within our financial boundaries. This not only maintained budgetary discipline but also fostered an atmosphere of transparency and inclusivity—key elements that keep the team motivated and engaged.

The model also guided us during larger investments, like when we considered buying video and camera equipment. This wasn't a spur-of-the-moment decision; it was calculated. Using our profitability framework, we determined the break-even point and decided to go ahead with the investment once we have secured five retainer clients who needed UGC as a retainer. Or even evaluating the need to setup inhouse podcast studio. This strategic approach allowed us to expand our offerings without jeopardizing financial stability and helped in enhancing our overall value for the clients.

Even when it came to hiring, the financial model provided much-needed clarity. Instead of reacting impulsively to workload pressures, we analyzed both current projects and future pipelines. This ensured that each new hire was a strategic choice, reinforcing our service delivery without overextending our resources.

AGILITY INDEX

As we scale smarter, one thing becomes clear—the ability to stay agile is what sets a thriving agency apart from the rest. This brings us to an essential element of financial growth: the agility index.

What the 30-20-50 model offered was the flexibility to adapt and expand strategically. This model allowed us to react quickly to market shifts while maintaining a strong financial foundation.

Your Launchpad for Growth: That 20 per cent contingency fund is your safety net; more than that, it's your ticket to seize new opportunities. Want to dive into the booming world of video marketing? That fund gives you the freedom to invest in equipment, software, or training without worrying about disrupting your operations. It's about making smart moves without putting your core business at risk, positioning you to scale when the time is right.

Do not hoard on to your contingency fund. Keep reinvesting it in to build and expand into newer and better avenue.

Growth That's Sustainable and Profitable: Growing your services sounds exciting, but it has to be smart. With the 30-20-50 model, you've got a clear path to sustainable growth. By using your contingency fund to bring on specialists or invest in new tools, you're not just expanding—you're doing it with purpose. Every decision is backed by solid financial reasoning, ensuring your moves are aligned with long-term profitability.

A Decision-Making Playbook: The real power of this model lies in its ability to help you make smarter decisions. Before jumping into any new venture, it forces you to pause and ask the tough questions: Will this investment bring in more revenue? Does this fit with the direction you want your agency to go? With this approach, you're not just reacting to the market—you're navigating it with a clear sense of purpose.

Having set down these golden rules for scaling your agency, it's time to share a little story about adaptability and resilience. Remember when having an office was almost like a badge of honour for an agency? Then came 2020, and suddenly, our living rooms became the new boardrooms. It was a curveball for sure, but also a lesson in disguise for us.

INNOVATION AMIDST CRISIS

When the pandemic hit, like many agencies, we had to think on our feet. The first big move was saying goodbye to our office space. It was a tough call, but guess what? It turned out to be a game-changer.

We pivoted to a remote setup, and with the money we saved on rent and utilities, we could invest in our team. Good internet, comfy chairs, and tech that made working from home a breeze became our new focus. It wasn't just about cutting costs; it was about showing the team we had their backs.

Facing the grim fact that 8 out of 10 digital agencies could shut down in their first year, we somehow managed to take a different path. When the pandemic hit, it really put us to the test, pushing many to the edge. But, thanks to our careful money management through the 30-20-50 profitability model, we came out stronger. We were quick to adapt, eager to innovate, and smart about using our resources. This helped us keep our operations solid and adapt quickly to market changes.

We kept growing our client list, made our team happier, and even tripled our revenue without upping our costs. Also, our emergency fund was a real game-changer, allowing us to keep our best people when things were still shaky. It felt like we'd cracked the code on not just getting by but actually thriving in uncertain times. This whole experience really highlighted how crucial it is to be prepared, flexible, and have a strong financial plan to make it through the tough times.

Our approach mirrored a global trend among digital agencies, who found that being asset-light didn't mean being ambition-light. On the contrary, it paved the way for a more agile, responsive business model that could easily adapt to changing market dynamics and client needs. This period of intense change demonstrated that the heart of any agency isn't its physical office but the creativity, resilience, and adaptability of its people.

The lessons learned during this time are invaluable for any agency founder. They underscore the importance of flexibility, the value of investing in your team, and the potential to scale and grow even in the face of unprecedented challenges.

GLOBAL GALLERY

Moz's Financial Playbook: From Blog to Big League

As we've worked through the ups and downs of managing finances in a digital agency, let's take a moment to expand our view with a real-world example from the global stage. I'm talking about Moz, a name many of us recognize in the world of SEO. Their financial journey offers some solid insights that can guide our own paths.

From Blog to Business: Moz's Early Days

Moz didn't start as the powerhouse software company we know today. It began as SEOmoz, a blog packed with SEO tips and advice. The early days were all about bootstrapping—using revenue from consulting services and blog monetization to keep the lights on and the wheels turning. What's important here is that Moz kept full control over their operations and decisions. They weren't answering to outside investors, which gave them the freedom to grow at their own pace, making decisions that aligned with their vision.

The Big Leap: Securing Venture Capital

Then came 2007, a game-changing year for Moz. They raised their first round of venture capital—$1.1 million. This wasn't just about having extra cash; it was about transforming from a consulting firm into a software company. This funding allowed Moz to build the Moz Pro SEO toolset, a product that would become their flagship offering. It also meant they could bring more people on board, scaling their team to meet the demands of their growing business.

Moz's success didn't go unnoticed. In 2012, they secured another $18 million, followed by $10 million in 2016. These funds were funneled into product development, marketing, and expanding their customer base. What's worth noting is how they did this without losing sight of sustainability. Every dollar was strategically invested to ensure they were growing with a purpose.

Moz's strategies closely mirrored the concepts discussed in the 30-20-50 profitability model. They reinvested profits back into the business—into product innovation and attracting new customers. And they did this while maintaining their company culture, ensuring that their team felt valued and motivated. This wasn't just about making money; it was about building a company that people wanted to work for and work with.

The road wasn't always smooth for Moz. As the SEO software market got more crowded, they faced stiff competition. But instead of panicking, they listened to their customers, refining their products based on real feedback. When Rand Fishkin, the founder, stepped down as CEO in 2014, and Sarah Bird took over, it was another moment of potential instability. But with careful financial planning, Moz stayed on course, continuing to innovate and grow.

So, what can you take away from Moz's journey? First, the importance of staying true to your values. Even as you grow, remember why you started in the first place. Second, be strategic with your finances—every investment should have a clear purpose. And finally, stay agile. The market will change, challenges will arise, but with the right mindset and planning, you can navigate through it all.

THE LEGAL EAGLE

After getting our ducks in a row with the whole money thing, there's another vital piece of the puzzle we need to fit in—legalities and company incorporation. I know, I know, just when you thought you'd escaped the clutches of complex jargon, here I am, pulling you back in. But stick with me; this is the good stuff, the kind that saves you from future headaches.

Now, setting up your agency is about making your vision official and giving it a legal identity. Think of it as the moment in superhero movies when the protagonist discovers their true identity. Exciting, right?

So, here's the lowdown on turning your agency from a dream into something that's legally recognised:

FLYING SOLO WITH PROPRIETORSHIP

If you're stepping into the digital marketing arena on your own, consider starting with a proprietorship. It's the simplest way to set sail, requiring less paperwork and giving you the freedom to steer in any direction you choose. But here's the catch: every decision, risk, and reward rests on your shoulders. If the business faces a storm (think debts or legal issues), your personal assets could be on the line.

CONSIDERING A PARTNERSHIP

If you have found the perfect partner who complements your digital marketing dreams, a partnership might be your best bet. It's like sharing the load of a hefty project, where both contribute skills, ideas, and resources. But remember to lay down clear rules of engagement to avoid any misunderstandings down the line. In a partnership, both parties share financial and legal responsibilities, making it essential to trust and communicate openly with your business partner.

SCALING BIG WITH A PRIVATE LIMITED COMPANY

Stepping up to a Private Limited Company could set the stage for growth if you are dreaming of making your agency a household name. This structure shields your personal assets from business risks, making it a safe haven as you aim for the stars. It's a bit more complex to navigate, with more rules to follow, but the perks, like attracting investment and limiting personal liability, are well worth it.

Each of these structures has its own set of pros and cons, tailored to different stages and styles of running your digital marketing agency. It's essential to choose a structure that fits your current situation and future goals. You're not locked into your initial choice forever. Many businesses start as sole proprietorships or partnerships and transition to a private limited company as they grow. This flexibility allows you to start small and scale up your legal structure as your business expands without overcomplicating things in the early stages.

Let's dive into a quick rundown of what each structure might mean for you, your business, and, yes, your peace of mind.

PROPRIETORSHIP

Pros	Cons
• Quick and straightforward to set up with minimal legal formalities. • Sole decision-making authority over the business operations and profits. • Benefits from lower tax rates and simpler tax filings. • Business affairs remain private, as there are no requirements to publicly disclose financials. • The owner enjoys all profits without needing to share.	• Personal assets are at risk if the business incurs debt or is sued. • Less credibility with banks and investors compared to a corporation. • Can be harder to scale significantly as a sole proprietor. • The business legally ceases to exist if the owner withdraws. • Managing every aspect of the business alone can be overwhelming.

PARTNERSHIP

Pros	Cons
• Partners can divide business tasks according to their strengths. • Greater potential for capital and resources than a sole proprietorship. • Combines the expertise and skills of all partners. • Profits are taxed as personal income, avoiding corporate tax rates. • Less paperwork and lower startup costs than corporations.	• Each partner is individually liable for business debts and decisions made by other partners. • Differences in vision or management style can lead to conflicts. • All profits must be shared among partners. • The partnership may dissolve if a partner decides to leave. • Changing ownership or selling a stake can be complicated and may require agreement from all partners.

PRIVATE LIMITED COMPANY

Pros	Cons
• Shareholders' personal assets are protected from business liabilities. • Easier to attract investment through the sale of shares. • The company continues to exist, even if ownership changes. • Potential for tax advantages and deductions not available to sole proprietorships or partnerships. • Often viewed more favourably by customers and suppliers.	• Subject to more regulations and compliance obligations. • Involves more paperwork and legal formalities than other structures. • Certain business information must be made public, reducing privacy. • Profits are typically distributed to shareholders in the form of dividends, which may be taxed. • Directors manage the company, potentially reducing the owner's control.

And there you have it—a whirlwind tour through the financial and legal foundations of setting up your digital marketing agency. We've broken down the numbers with the 30-20-50 Profitability Model, dug into smart spending strategies for scaling, and explored how the Financial Growth Tree keeps everything rooted and thriving. We've also tackled the legal landscape, from proprietorships to private limited companies, ensuring you're set up for long-term success. It's like we've laid the groundwork, brick by brick, so when you build, you're building on solid ground, not shifting sand.

As we go ahead, remember these wise words: "The best time to plant a tree was 20 years ago. The second best time is now." It's never too late to get your financial and legal ducks in a row, setting the stage for growth, innovation, and success.

CHAPTER 7

IRONING OUT THE CREASES

Have you ever thought about your agency as a sophisticated engine of a high-performance vehicle? I've grown to appreciate this parallel ever since the early days of running my own digital marketing agency. And when I chat with fellow marketers, they nod in agreement because, let's face it—your agency really is like an engine. Regular tuning and a clear understanding of how every cog turns are what keep the whole system humming. That's where processes come into play.

Processes might not have the glitz and glam of flashy marketing campaigns, but they're the behind-the-scenes rockstars that power every operation. Think about those days when your team clicks perfectly, and projects flow seamlessly from concept to completion. This is the magic of well-oiled processes at work. W. Edwards Deming, the legendary American economist, couldn't have put it better: "If you can't describe what you are doing as a process, you don't know what you're doing." This idea really resonates in the hustle and bustle of a digital marketing agency, where getting your processes down pat is key.

In the beginning, it's normal to encounter a few bumps as you try to set effective processes. It's essential to fine-tune these early on. Without careful attention to how all the parts work together, your agency's engine is at risk of breaking down mid-journey. And that's a situation no one wants to find themselves in.

So, why wait for the wheels to come off? Let's dive into what it takes to keep your agency running smoothly, like a well-oiled machine, ready to cruise ahead of the competition.

Streamlining Workflows in Your Digital Marketing Agency

Think of your agency as a finely tuned machine, where every cog—from content creation to client onboarding—needs to work in sync to keep things running smoothly. When each component operates seamlessly, the whole system delivers top-tier performance, pushing your agency ahead of the competition.

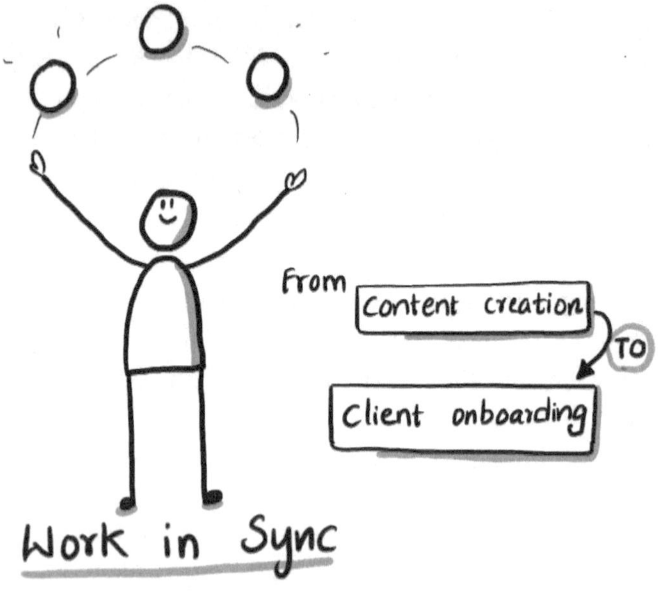

Blueprint for Precision

To get your machine running at full capacity, start by defining and documenting your workflows. Whether it's SEO, social media management, or client onboarding, every step matters. By creating Standard Operating Procedures (SOPs), you give your team a reliable playbook that details roles, timelines, and quality standards. This ensures consistency and efficiency—crucial for scaling your operations smoothly.

The Oil for Your Gears

Without effective communication, even the best machine grinds to a halt. Platforms like Slack and Microsoft Teams centralize your agency's communication, ensuring that no one misses a beat. Regular check-ins are like quick pit stops—keeping everyone aligned, informed, and ready for the next move. Consistent communication helps avoid breakdowns and keeps projects moving forward with precision.

Fueling Your Team's Performance

Think of resource allocation as your fuel gauge—keeping everything running smoothly while preventing burnout. Tools like Resource Guru or Float help you manage your team's capacity, ensuring that tasks are distributed efficiently and no one is overburdened. By keeping a close eye on your resources, you ensure that your agency never runs out of fuel, maintaining peak performance at all times.

The Master Cog that Ties It All Together

Here's the secret that ties every cog in this machine together—automation. By automating routine tasks and streamlining your workflows, you keep the entire machine running like clockwork. Whether it's automating emails, project updates, or task management, automation helps reduce manual errors, speeds up processes, and lets you focus on scaling your agency efficiently.

As we work on optimizing your workflows, remember that creating an SOP checklist is essential. It will help your agency run smoothly and efficiently, just like it's supposed to.

THE ESSENTIAL SOP CHECKLIST

As you refine your agency's processes, a set of well-defined Standard Operating Procedures (SOPs) becomes essential. SOPs streamline your operations, ensuring consistency, efficiency, and smooth communication across every part of your agency. Let's break down a must-have checklist for setting up your agency's SOPs, from creative workflows to legal and financial processes.

CONSISTENCY MEETS INNOVATION

The creative engine drives your agency forward. But creativity without structure can lead to chaos. A solid Creative SOP ensures your team knows the steps from concept to delivery, with clear guidelines for approvals and revisions. It's about maintaining the balance between inspiration and efficiency, so every campaign reflects your client's vision without missing a beat.

PROTECTING THE FOUNDATION

Legal procedures are the bedrock of your agency's stability. Having clear Legal SOPs helps you navigate contracts, client agreements, and any potential disputes. It also ensures that you stay compliant with industry standards and advertising laws.

POWERING GROWTH

Finance is the engine that powers your agency's scalability. A well-documented Finance SOP keeps invoicing, budget tracking, and expense management clear and simple. It ensures you're always financially sound and ready for the next big opportunity without getting bogged down by cash flow headaches.

A SMOOTH TAKEOFF

Starting a project without a plan is like taking a flight without a destination. Your Project Initiation SOP sets the course for every project, from kickoff meetings to assigning roles and setting deadlines. It ensures that everyone is on the same page from day one, creating a seamless flow from client onboarding to the final delivery.

KEEPING THE PEACE

Even in the most well-oiled agencies, conflicts happen. A conflict resolution SOP outlines the steps for resolving disputes, whether internal or client-related. By having this in place, you ensure that disagreements are handled professionally, preventing them from derailing progress.

Together, these SOPs form the backbone of your agency's operations. They ensure that every part of your agency works in harmony.

MASTERING PROJECT DELIVERY

With your SOP checklists in place, your agency's engine is now primed to run at peak performance. But what comes next is where your agency truly gets to shine—delivering projects with impact. It all starts with setting clear, measurable goals. Whether you're aiming to boost conversion rates or increase engagement, knowing exactly what you're targeting is like entering the destination in your GPS before setting out. Once those goals are defined, use project management tools like Asana or Trello to map out each step. A solid plan not only keeps everyone on task but also ensures that deadlines are met and nothing falls through the cracks.

As the project progresses, real-time data is your compass. Tools like Google Analytics or SEMrush help you stay on course, providing the insights needed to tweak your strategy along the way. Think of it as A/B testing different paths until you find the one that leads to success. Some approaches will hit the mark, while others might need a little adjusting, but that's all part of refining your strategy for maximum impact.

Communication is the glue that holds everything together. Whether your team is brainstorming in person or working remotely, tools like Slack ensure everyone stays in the loop. Regular check-ins act like team huddles, keeping the momentum going and ensuring all team members are aligned and motivated.

And finally, before you launch, don't skimp on the polish. Thorough reviews and testing are crucial to ensure that every detail aligns with the client's vision. Involve them in the feedback process—after all, collaboration leads to refinement, and that extra input can turn a good project into something truly exceptional.

As we work on making our project delivery better, it's important to also be ready for surprises. Things don't always go as planned, and being prepared for anything is key. I remember once when a key team member left out of the blue in the middle of a big project. It could have been a huge mess, but instead, it showed how strong and flexible our team is. We all came together, split up the work, and supported each other to overcome the challenge. This incident really highlighted how crucial it is to have solid backup plans in place. It also showed off the resilience that's at the heart of our team. Adopting this proactive and effective approach to delivering projects can truly cement your agency's reputation as a dependable and innovative force, fully capable of bringing visions to life, even in the face of unexpected challenges.

STREAMLINING THE CLIENT HANDOVER PROCESS

As we're rounding off the project delivery phase, it's important to make sure your client has a smooth handover. This is about setting your clients up to really succeed and make the most of the final product. Let's talk about how to hand over the reins smoothly, so your clients feel ready and confident to take charge.

The comprehensive and clear documentation serves as a light house for the clients.

Ready, Set, Prep

Before you even think about handing off the project, make sure every detail is locked in. Create clear, comprehensive documentation that includes everything your client will need—think project scope, deliverables, timelines, and contact info. Throw in user guides, training materials, and access credentials for good measure. This will be their reference manual, so make it crystal clear. Before finalizing, run through an internal review to confirm all is in top shape and aligned with your agency's standards.

The Big Handoff

Prepare a solid agenda for the handover meeting that covers both the big picture and all the nitty-gritty details. Give your client a walkthrough of the deliverables and show them how everything ties back to their goals. Most importantly, ensure they know how to use any tools or platforms that come with the package. Tailor the training to match their comfort level with tech, ensuring they feel confident navigating the systems you've provided.

We've Got Your Back

Just because the project is handed over doesn't mean your work is done. Set up a post-handover support plan so the client knows exactly where to go if they need help. Outline your support response times and any extra services they might need. Also, don't forget to schedule follow-ups. These check-ins help smooth out any wrinkles, making sure the client is comfortable with everything and reinforcing that long-term relationship.

When you nail each step of this handover process, you're equipping your client for long-term success and satisfaction, ensuring they're ready to thrive.

THE FINAL REPORT

After a detailed client handover, we move into a critical phase that really puts our work in the spotlight: final reporting. Think of this as the grand reveal, where we lay all our cards on the table to show just how much impact our strategies have had. To tell a compelling story with data, start by setting up a clear analytics dashboard using tools like Google Data Studio or Klipfolio. These platforms turn raw numbers into insights, transforming web traffic spikes and changes in customer acquisition costs into a cohesive narrative.

Monthly and quarterly reports keep the momentum going. These reviews allow you to celebrate wins, identify areas for improvement, and adjust strategies to keep things moving in the right direction.

Of course, feedback plays a huge role. Establishing a system to collect and act on feedback ensures your strategies stay fresh and client-focused. It's a loop of continuous improvement—every piece of feedback makes your next move stronger.

When it comes to structuring the final report, think of it as the final showcase of your work. Start with an executive summary that captures the highlights and key takeaways. Dive deeper with detailed analysis, explaining the significance of the results for your client's business. Use visuals to make complex data more digestible, and top it off with actionable recommendations that spark conversations about future strategies. The aim is to show your client not just what you did, but how it will continue to deliver returns.

We have spoken at length about developing and refining the operations of your organization. Now, let's zoom out to see the bigger picture. To ensure that all parts of your agency work together well, it's essential to focus on a few more critical aspects. You can't have one part of your agency functioning well while another part is completely defunct. This is where two crucial pillars come into play: Team Cohesion and Efficient Backend Operations. Let's delve into each, starting with team cohesion.

TEAM COHESION: THE SECRET SAUCE OF AGENCY SUCCESS

Building a cohesive team is crucial to any agency's success, and it starts with keeping everyone in sync. Regular team meetings create a space for discussing ongoing projects, sharing updates, and solving problems together. These meetings keep everyone informed, aligned, and engaged in collective problem-solving.

Incorporating tools like Slack or Microsoft Teams makes real-time communication seamless. These platforms keep discussions organized and accessible, ensuring no one is left out. Pair that with structured feedback mechanisms, like anonymous surveys, and you create a steady stream of insights on improving collaboration.

Team-building is equally important. Workshops and retreats centered around trust-building and creative brainstorming can strengthen bonds. In our agency, we noticed a disconnect between our content creators and designers, so we launched brainstorming sessions specifically for them. These "creative jams" brought fresh ideas, smoothed communication, and ultimately, elevated our projects.

Clear role definitions are essential to prevent overlaps and ensure each team member knows what's expected. An organizational chart can help everyone understand how they fit into the bigger picture. Combine that with project management tools like Asana or Monday.com to assign tasks and track progress. These platforms act as the team's roadmap, reducing confusion and keeping everyone accountable.

Cloud-based document sharing tools like Google Drive or Dropbox also play a key role. These digital "filing cabinets" allow for real-time collaboration, keeping everyone on the same page without endless email threads.

Regular training fosters continuous growth, making learning a core part of your agency's culture. Encourage cross-training so team members can gain a deeper understanding of different roles, boosting versatility and collaboration. Finally, addressing conflicts early is key to maintaining harmony. Think of it as routine maintenance on your vehicle. Sometimes, bringing in a third-party mediator can offer a fresh perspective, helping bridge gaps and forge solutions that are acceptable to all involved.

When you use these strategies, you're making sure every part of your agency is absolutely thriving. Keep in mind, being a well-oiled machine is not about having the best parts. It's all about getting them to work together in perfect harmony.

Once you've made sure all parts of your agency are perfectly aligned, it's also important to pay attention to the backend elements. They're key to keeping your team united.

AUTOMATING REPETITIVE TASKS TO BOOST EFFICIENCY

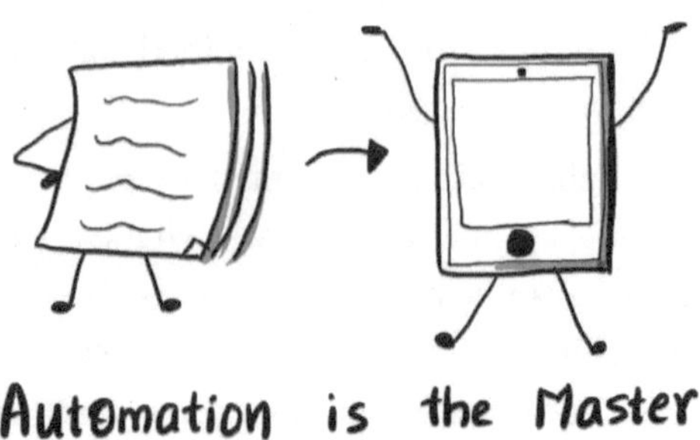

Automation is the master cog that ties all the parts of your agency's workflow together. Just like we discussed earlier, where each part of the workflow is a cog that needs to work together, automation ensures those cogs spin smoothly, freeing up your team from repetitive tasks to focus on strategy and creativity.

For example, using automation tools for lead nurturing can take over repetitive follow-ups. Tools like Zapier connect your CRM to email marketing platforms like Mailchimp, ensuring no lead slips through the cracks—just as each cog moves the next, automating these touchpoints keeps the entire process flowing without manual intervention. It's part of the larger system that keeps your operations running seamlessly.

On the financial side, automation helps keep the engine running smoothly. Platforms like QuickBooks or FreshBooks handle invoicing and expense tracking with little oversight, while tools like Moon Invoice and Stripe ensure payments are processed and tracked, fitting into the larger workflow of keeping financials aligned with your business goals.

In our agency, automating routine accounting tasks was transformative. It allowed our team to shift their focus from day-to-day management to strategic growth, aligning perfectly with the operational efficiencies we've built.

Elevate Your Data Game

Think about all the client information you handle daily. Managing this data effectively is crucial for both operational efficiency and security. By setting up robust data management systems, you ensure that all client data is well-organized and securely protected from unauthorized access. This setup is about safeguarding the lifeblood of your business and maintaining trust.

Consistent data backups are equally important. Regularly backing up your data means that in the face of a system failure or a cyberattack, your agency can quickly bounce back without losing precious information. It's about continuity and resilience, ensuring that no matter what happens, your agency remains up and running.

The Power of Proactive Communication

Proactive communication is key to client satisfaction. Integrating a Customer Relationship Management (CRM) system like Salesforce or HubSpot can transform how you track and manage client interactions. These systems organize all communication, making sure you're always on top of client needs and project timelines. It's about being responsive and proactive—qualities that can set your agency apart in a competitive market.

Client portals offer another layer of transparency and engagement. By giving clients access to a portal where they can see project updates, reports, and other relevant information, you enhance their experience. They're not just observing from the sidelines; they're actively involved, which can significantly boost their satisfaction and trust in your services.

Grow Without the Glitches

As your agency grows, your infrastructure must evolve too. Investing in scalable, cloud-based solutions means that as your workload increases, your systems can handle it smoothly without the need for a complete overhaul. This scalability ensures that your agency can grow without being hampered by technological limitations.

Flexible processes are also vital. They allow your agency to adapt quickly to changes in client demands or market conditions. This agility is crucial—it means you can pivot as needed without missing a beat, staying relevant and effective no matter the situation.

Focusing on these areas improves your agency's operational efficiency, enhances client satisfaction, and prepares your business for growth and new challenges.

As we wrap up our exploration of backend efficiency, remember that creating effective processes for your agency is an ongoing journey. It's like laying bricks while walking backwards—requiring both foresight and flexibility.

In your agency's first year, aim to strike a balance. Avoid over-engineering your systems, as too many rigid processes can stifle creativity and slow you down. Focus instead on establishing essential procedures that streamline operations and support your team's efficiency. These foundational processes can often be standardized as SOPs, providing a stable structure for your daily functions.

At the same time, give other processes the space to evolve naturally. These will become the cultural backbone of your organization, shaping how your team collaborates and how your agency grows.

Consider this early phase as preparing the soil for future growth. Just as a gardener prepares the ground to nurture a variety of plants, you must create an environment where flexible, effective processes can thrive. This preparation ensures your agency remains agile and adaptable, ready to tackle new challenges and seize opportunities.

GLOBAL GALLERY

360i: Mastering Operational Excellence

As we wrap up our exploration of backend operations, let's peer across the globe for an example that embodies these principles in action. Who better to learn from than 360i, a pioneer in the digital marketing world?

Founded in 1998 in the streets of New York City, 360i started as a search engine marketing and technology firm. Over the years, it has blossomed into a full-service digital agency, mastering a spectrum of services from social media marketing to mobile marketing, and beyond. Today, 360i stands as a paragon of innovation and effectiveness in the digital marketing industry.

Streamlining for Success

The story of 360i's operational success begins with a critical look at their existing workflows.The problem was all too common: outdated content approval processes that slowed projects to a crawl with endless email chains and clunky spreadsheet tracking. This often led to lost content and annoying delays.

Simplifying Processes with SOPs

360i tackled these challenges head-on by developing and implementing Standard Operating Procedures (SOPs) across the board. These SOPs were about creating a blueprint that made daily tasks quicker and more consistent, significantly reducing the time spent on routine processes.

Empowering Through Engagement

What truly set 360i apart was their approach to employee involvement. Change wasn't handed down from above; it was shaped with insights from the people who would interact with these new systems every single day. The training sessions became transformative experiences, crafted to make sure that every team member was embracing and advocating for the new procedures.

The Power of Expion

360i teamed up with Expion, a top-notch social media management software company, taking a huge tech step forward. They streamlined how content is created, approved, and analyzed, cutting down the usual time spent on these tasks. Thanks to Expion's platform, community managers could quickly get content ready, speeding up client approvals by an incredible 90per cent.

Embracing Automation and Data Analytics

The agency took it a step further by diving into automation and advanced data analytics tools. This move by 360i was about revolutionizing how they worked. By adopting these technologies, they were able to identify and fix process bottlenecks and fine-tune their workflows. The real magic happened when they shifted their focus from the mundane task of gathering data to creating insightful analytic reports. This transition transformed how they made strategic decisions, ultimately leading to better results for their clients.

Refining Client Relationships with Advanced CRM Systems

When 360i rolled out a sophisticated CRM system, it revolutionized their approach to client interactions. Suddenly, they had their fingers on the pulse of customer behavior with real-time updates and deeper insights, leading to a significant boost in service quality and efficiency. This paved the way for marketing campaigns that hit closer to home, driving up engagement and sales in the process.

The integration of new technologies led to a significant boost in efficiency and productivity. 360i could now complete tasks faster, reduce expenses, and increase output, freeing up the team to focus on creative and strategic efforts. This leap in operational quality caught the attention of big names like Google, who saw the value in 360i's ability to enhance online content and improve search engine rankings. 360i's journey was far from over once they hit operational excellence. They constantly pushed the envelope, making sure to regularly review and refresh their processes and technologies. This dedication kept them at the forefront of the digital marketing world, always delivering top-notch value to their clients.

The journey of 360i has shown us that a deep commitment to operational excellence can truly transform an agency. When you start applying these lessons, you're creating a resilient, dynamic environment that's all about embracing innovation and efficiency.

Think of this as laying down the vital roots that will support your agency's growth, enabling you to adapt swiftly and effectively to whatever new challenges or opportunities the digital world might throw your way.

CHAPTER 8

SURVIVAL OF THE FITTEST

Today's world is zooming by so fast, where the only constant is change. The way our current tech keeps morphing and new stuff keeps popping up - from AI tools to brand-new media platforms - it feels like we're living in a whirlwind of change. Have you ever wondered what keeps a digital marketing agency afloat and successful in this super speedy world? Look through the pages we've explored together, and you'll spot the answer: adaptability. Charles Darwin famously said, *"It is not the strongest of the species that survives, nor the most intelligent. It is the one that is most adaptable to change."*

The similarity between nature and digital strategy is no accident. Just like in the wild, the key to success in the digital world is being able to change and grow with your surroundings. Think of your agency as a living thing in the vast digital space. Every time there's a new algorithm update or a shift in what people like, it's an opportunity for you to evolve. How you react to these changes and how well you can tweak your strategies and come up with new ideas will decide your spot in the digital world.

It's all about turning challenges into opportunities and making the most of what we've got to thrive. So, let's dive into how being adaptable in the digital scene can make a big difference, with some real-life examples.

So, let me rewind to the early days of Instagram Stories for a second. Many were skeptical, preferring the familiar terrain of traditional posts. Yet, in my agency, we sensed an opportunity in this fleeting, yet captivating format. We launched experimental campaigns—offering a glimpse behind the scenes, unveiling new products, and engaging audiences with interactive polls. The response was beyond our expectations: a surge in engagement and an increase in followers. This adaptability kept our clients ahead of the curve and solidified our reputation as forward-thinking marketers.

Now, let's talk about how you can implement similar strategies to integrate adaptability into the core of your digital marketing agency, making it as natural as breathing.

Learn to Grow

Motivate your team to dive into courses, participate in webinars, and chase certifications. Companies like Google and HubSpot provide complimentary courses to keep your abilities honed and current. Here's a snapshot from our playbook: every Friday, our team dedicates an hour to a "learning session" where we share nuggets of wisdom from the most recent course or webinar we've explored. It can be both fun and incredibly enriching.

Trend Surfing

Leverage tools like Google Trends, BuzzSumo, and social media listening platforms to keep a pulse on the next big thing. Take TikTok's rise, for example. We immediately recognized its appeal to younger audiences and harnessed that by crafting engaging content for a fashion brand, catapulting them to viral status and significantly ramping up their sales.

Dynamic Agility

Agility thrives on the power to move with speed and precision. Embrace agile methodologies, such as daily stand-ups and sprint planning, and watch your agency become a nimble force, ready to pivot with the shifting demands of the market and your clients. Think of breaking down vast projects into bite-sized tasks - it's like giving your team the ability to zero in on delivering value bit by bit, inspring a culture of steady progress and flexibility. Regular check-ins open doors for feedback and tweaks, ensuring projects stay aligned with client objectives. It's about embracing flexibility and readiness, so when changes arise, your team isn't caught off guard—they're equipped and prepared.

Refining through Client Echoes

Hearing your clients out is a strategic must. Dive into regular feedback sessions, and watch as your services transform, becoming a closer fit to what your clients really want and expect. Why not tweak your campaign strategies on the fly, guided by the honest feedback you get? It leads to happier clients and sharper results. This kind of proactive engagement inspires innovation, ensuring your services grow in ways that truly click with your clients.

Tech It Up a Notch

Technology revolutionizes digital marketing. Jumping on the latest tools, from sophisticated CRM systems to groundbreaking analytics platforms, can dramatically boost your operational efficiency and strategic intelligence. These innovations allow you to hand off the tedious tasks to machines, giving your team the freedom to dive into more creative and strategic projects. Consider harnessing the power of AI-driven analytics to delve into the nuances of consumer behavior. This approach enables you to craft campaigns that resonate on a deeper level and lead to meaningful conversions. By keeping your finger on the pulse of technological advancements, your agency stands out by offering cutting-edge solutions that capture interest and deliver quantifiable outcomes.

All the above are interconnected elements that create a solid framework of adaptability for your agency. This approach ensures that you are always prepared to adapt, innovate, and set the pace in the digital race.

THE ART OF ADAPTATION: LESSONS FROM OUR DIGITAL JOURNEY

As you think about bringing this framework into your digital marketing agency, let me share the insights we've gained from integrating these elements into our own story. Our commitment to staying adaptable allowed us to embrace these lessons and document them for you.

One of the most critical insights we've embraced is the importance of flexibility. In the digital space, where new trends and technologies emerge almost daily, sticking rigidly to a plan simply doesn't work. For example, when a major social media platform overhauled its algorithm unexpectedly, we didn't descend into chaos. We quickly tweaked our strategies and content plans, ensuring our clients remained visible and engaged. This experience highlighted the importance of having flexible plans that can pivot instantly.

As we journeyed further into our digital adventure, we've unearthed a crucial truth: letting data guide our decisions is key to sharpening our strategies. Initially, we relied on gut feelings and the lessons of the past. While this approach had its moments, we quickly recognized the undeniable value of grounding our strategies in solid data. Take, for instance, our work on optimizing a client's landing pages. Diving deep into the ebb and flow of their website traffic, we crafted targeted tweaks that sparked a 25per cent jump in conversions. This shift to embracing data sharpened our decision-making and supercharged its impact.

At the same time, we've doubled down on our promise to always put our clients first. By really getting to the heart of what our clients need, we've managed to build deeper and lasting connections. I remember a particular project where the client decided to shift their campaign focus midway. The shift came out of nowhere, but our knack for tuning in and swiftly shifting gears to match their fresh goals met their expectations and strengthened our collaboration. This flexibility has become our secret weapon in meeting client needs and transforming hurdles into stepping stones for growth.

Our dedication to investing in technology has been just as important. I remember the key decision to invest in an advanced analytics tool, which was a big financial step for us at the time. The insights we gained from this tool completely changed the game for us. This experience opened our eyes like never before, helping us get a crystal-clear picture of who our audience really is. We honed our targeting techniques and saw our campaign results soar. It was a real lesson in the value of dedicating a slice of our budget to adopting new tech that amps up our game. Keeping pace with the newest tools, we sharpen our competitive edge, making sure our strategies are both powerful and enlightened.

It's this combination that keeps us adaptable and agile, ready to tackle whatever new challenges come our way.

THE FUTURE IS NOW

Having laid out our core principles and the unique blend of elements we bring to the table, I want to focus on a point we touched on last - our investment and adoption of new technologies. In the digital-first world we're living in, this is absolutely crucial. Let me explain why.

Stepping Ahead with New Tech

Diving into emerging tech puts you ahead of the curve. Consider integrating AI, blockchain, and cutting-edge analytics into the fabric of your operations. Blockchain is a fast lane to building trust with your clients. Embracing these innovations early not only marks you as a trailblazer but also distinguishes you from the pack, proving your agency is a leader that dares to lead, not just follow.

Innovating with Purpose

Why stick to the old when you can innovate with the new? Technologies like virtual reality (VR) provide immersive experiences that can transform how your audience interacts with your brand. For example, using VR to showcase a new product gives customers a hands-on experience from anywhere in the world, skyrocketing engagement and driving up conversion rates. It's this kind of innovation that keeps your offerings exciting and, more crucially, deeply relevant.

Enhancing Efficiency, Reducing Costs

The initial investment in technology might look steep, but the efficiencies it brings are undeniable. Take AI and automation, for instance—these are tools to reduce manual labor, optimize your resources and cut down long-term operational costs. Automation in email marketing or customer segmentation frees up your team's time for creative and strategic tasks, enhancing productivity while maintaining high standards of delivery.

Understanding Your Impact

When we tap into advanced analytics and the latest technologies, we're crunching numbers and building stronger bonds with our clients. These tools allow us to present clear, measurable results that demonstrate the effectiveness of our campaigns and foster trust. It's about showing how our efforts translate into real success for our clients. This kind of transparency makes your agency an indispensable partner, not merely a service provider.

Personal Touch

Imagine having a tool that tells you exactly what your clients need, even before they ask. That's the power of AI-enhanced CRM systems. They analyze patterns and preferences, allowing us to tailor our approach to each client's unique requirements. This provides a personalized experience that makes clients feel valued and understood, increasing their loyalty and satisfaction with our work.

Adapt to the
AI driven world.

Future -Proofing Your Agency

Investing in new technologies might seem daunting, but it's an essential step towards future-proofing your agency. By embracing innovations early, we prepare ourselves to respond to future trends and lead the way. This proactive stance helps us stay relevant and competitive, providing services that are current and pioneering.

As we explore technology's role in future-proofing our agency and staying ahead, let's address the elephant in the room, which can actually be a very useful tool for us—AI.

You've probably heard rumors about AI being the boogeyman of the job market, especially in creative industries like ours. But let me tell you, that's not the full story. AI isn't here to replace us; it's becoming an integral part of how we work, enhancing our capabilities rather than diminishing our roles. Embracing AI means staying relevant, and those who adapt are the ones who thrive.

Take it from our own experience at the agency. Integrating AI didn't cut jobs; it revolutionized them. By automating the monotonous, time-consuming tasks, our team shifted its focus to deep strategy and creative innovation. Imagine cutting down the hours spent on data crunching and using that time to brainstorm groundbreaking campaigns—this is the reality AI has unlocked for us.

SELLING AI AS A SERVICE

Many traditional businesses are struggling to adapt to the fast-paced, AI-driven world. They don't have the time, expertise, or tools to keep up with constant changes. This is where your agency comes into play, providing AI as a service that bridges this gap and establishes you as a vital partner in their growth. From predictive analytics to content automation, businesses are looking for agencies that already have this knowledge and can deliver solutions that keep them competitive. The future belongs to agencies that can guide clients through these AI advancements, from HubSpot integrations to LinkedIn videos, without missing a beat. No AI can replace the value of a forward-thinking, agile agency.

HERE'S HOW YOU CAN SELL AI AS A SERVICE:

Tailoring with Precision: Offering Hyper-Personalized Campaigns AI's ability to deliver personalized experiences is a game-changer, and you can use this to help your clients speak directly to their audience. For instance, we leveraged AI to analyze audience data for a client, allowing us to craft targeted email campaigns that increased engagement by 20per cent. Businesses are eager to adopt this level of personalization, but they often don't know where to start. This is where your agency steps in—providing precision-driven, AI-powered campaigns that drive results.

Predictive Analytics: Forecasting Future Success Position predictive analytics as a service that offers businesses a clear look into the future. We used AI's predictive power to forecast campaign performance for a client, tweaking budgets and strategies ahead of time. When a product's demand spiked, we were ready, and sales surged. Offering predictive analytics as part of your AI service empowers businesses to make smarter, data-backed decisions, giving them the edge they need in an unpredictable market.

AI as Your Content Collaborator: Content creation is a heavy lift for many businesses. Offering AI-powered content generation as a service can revolutionize the way your clients create and manage their marketing efforts. For example, AI helped us generate blog topics and draft social media posts with ease. Businesses need this support—they don't have the bandwidth to maintain a steady stream of fresh content. With AI, you become their creative collaborator, ensuring they never miss a beat in their content strategy.

Smart Spending: AI-Powered Ad Optimization Businesses are always looking to make their advertising dollars work harder, and you can provide AI-driven ad optimization as part of your service package. We've used AI tools to automatically adjust bids and budgets in real time, achieving a 15per cent drop in cost-per-click and a 10per cent increase in conversions for one of our clients. Offering AI-based ad management shows your clients that their campaigns are efficient and constantly evolving to maximize ROI.

Understanding the Pulse of Your Audience: Sentiment analysis is like having a real-time pulse check on how people feel about your brand. . AI tools can sift through customer feedback, online reviews, and social media mentions to gauge the public mood. This is invaluable when it comes to spotting potential problems before they spiral out of control. For example, we once used sentiment analysis to detect a brewing PR issue for a client. With that early warning, we could act fast, resolving the issue and protecting the brand's reputation before it hit the fan. Offering sentiment analysis as part of your service keeps clients ahead of crises, maintaining their brand image and keeping trust intact.

Adoption of new technologies is crucial.

Your 24/7 Customer Service Reps: Picture having a customer service team that's always available—day or night—without the overhead costs. AI-powered chatbots can provide this, offering instant, helpful responses around the clock. We rolled out a chatbot for one of our client's e-commerce platforms, and it was a game-changer. Not only did it handle common customer queries and reduce support tickets, but it also recommended products, boosting sales. The result? Happier customers and a more efficient team. By offering chatbots as a service, you can help businesses keep their customers engaged and satisfied, while also freeing up their human team to handle more complex tasks.

Automate the Journey

Let me give you an insider's view on how automating the customer journey, particularly through AI-powered tools and selling AI as a service, became a major learning experience for us.

THE BEGINNING OF OUR AUTOMATION JOURNEY

Our first step was thorough research and careful selection. We sifted through various automation platforms, seeking one that was both user-friendly and compatible with our client's existing digital infrastructure. Finding the right solution felt like searching for a needle in a haystack—lots of features to compare, countless reviews to read. But after sleepless nights of deliberation, we landed on the perfect match, one that promised seamless integration and smooth functionality.

TEAM TRAINING

Next came team training, where we approached the process with the same excitement as learning a new language, knowing it could transform the way we managed customer interactions. Our team was trained to create automation scripts that tackled common customer queries, guiding users through the sales funnel and ensuring they moved from casual visitors to satisfied customers with minimal friction.

ROLLING OUT AUTOMATION

Deploying the automation tools on our client's website felt like the start of a new journey. We tested rigorously to ensure every function worked smoothly. Of course, it wasn't without its early hiccups—some queries stumped the system at first, leading to amusing yet valuable lessons. With every test, we refined responses, smoothing out the kinks until the automation ran as naturally as a human conversation.

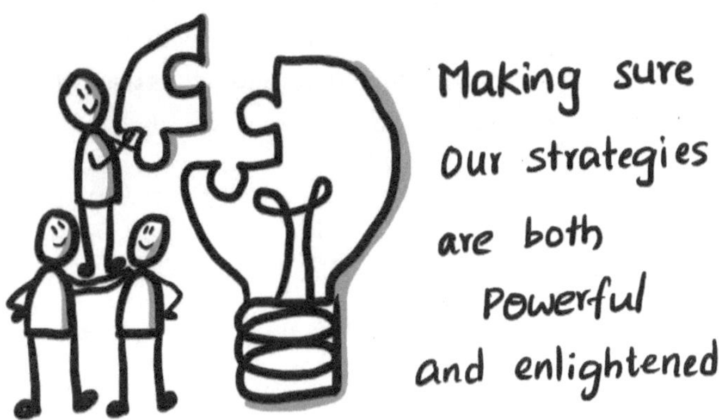

MONITORING FOR CONTINUOUS SUCCESS

The real test began when we moved into the crucial phase of monitoring and optimizing. This involved analyzing every interaction to fine-tune the system and push it beyond expectations. The effort paid off when our client saw a remarkable 30per cent spike in lead conversions. This wasn't just a win—it was proof that the automation we had set up was effectively enhancing customer interactions.

SUSTAINED IMPROVEMENTS AND CLIENT DELIGHT

The results were clear: customer satisfaction soared as queries were handled efficiently, and potential customers received fast, accurate responses. Casual website visitors were transformed into engaged prospects, boosting conversion rates significantly. Both we and our client were thrilled with the results.

Automating the journey, as we've learned, involves continuous learning, fine-tuning, and ensuring that the technology operates as smoothly as possible to continually enhance the customer experience. With that in mind, let's move on to exploring the future technologies and trends that will keep your agency at the forefront.

HOW TO CHOOSE WINNING TECHNOLOGIES FOR YOUR AGENCY

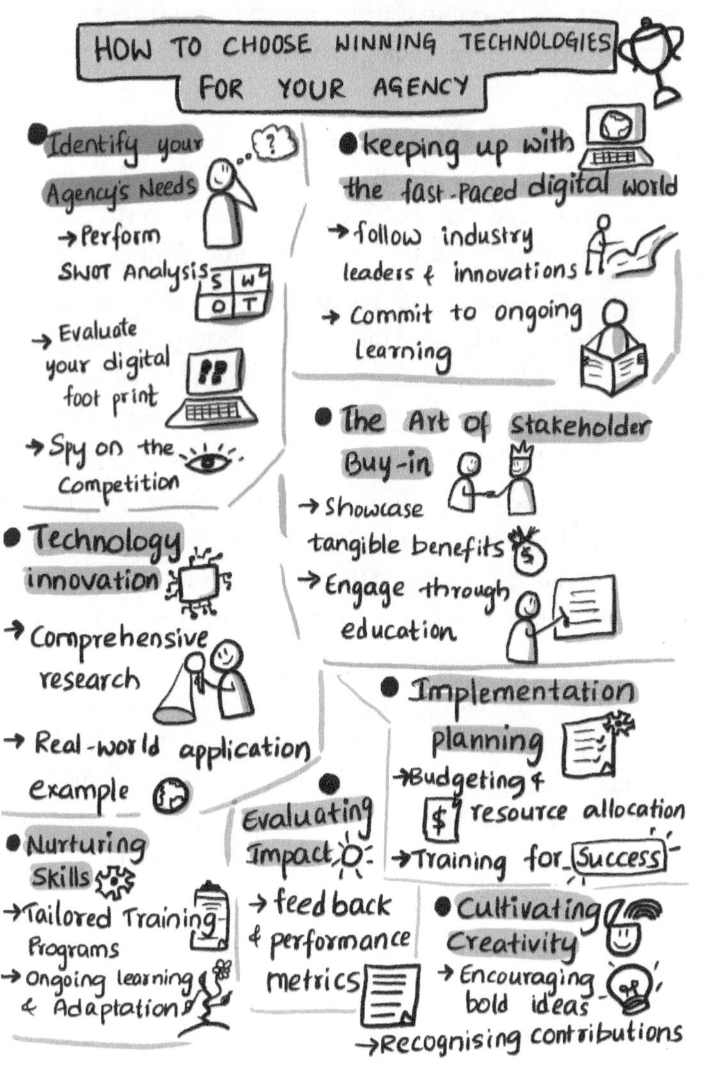

IDENTIFYING YOUR AGENCY'S NEEDS

Let's start with a groundwork exercise—a comprehensive needs assessment. It's crucial to clarify what you need before you can effectively scout for technology solutions. Here's how you can kick this off:

Perform a SWOT Analysis: Get a clear picture of where your agency stands by identifying your Strengths, Weaknesses, Opportunities, and Threats. This will not only help you leverage your strong points but also address any vulnerabilities.

Evaluate Your Digital Footprint: Take a thorough look at your current digital tactics. How is your website performing? Are your social media strategies engaging enough? What about the ROI on your email campaigns? Understanding these elements will pinpoint what's working and what needs a tech upgrade.

Spy on the Competition: Sometimes, keeping an eye on your competition gives you the best insights. What tech are they using? How are they engaging their audience? By understanding these, you can identify technological gaps in your own strategy and find ways to outpace your competitors.

For example, let's say you find out through this assessment that your current analytics tools are underperforming, especially when handling large sets of data. This revelation could steer you towards more robust, AI-enhanced analytics platforms, tailored to manage big data efficiently and with more precision.

KEEPING UP WITH THE FAST-PACED DIGITAL WORLD

Staying updated with the latest trends is a must. Here's how you can keep your finger on the pulse of the digital marketing world:

Follow Industry Leaders and Innovations: Immerse yourself in the wealth of knowledge available through blogs, webinars, and leading digital publications. Places like Digital Marketing Institute and CMSWire are goldmines for trends predictions and tech updates.

Commit to Ongoing Learning: Encourage your team to engage in continuous learning. Whether it's attending flagship industry events like HubSpot's INBOUND conference or enrolling in online courses that focus on emerging tech like AI, blockchain, or the latest in data analytics.

THE ART OF STAKEHOLDER BUY-IN

To effectively integrate new technologies into your digital marketing agency, it's essential to have your stakeholders aligned and enthusiastic. Here's how you can secure their buy-in:

Showcase Tangible Benefits: Clearly articulate the advantages these technologies will bring. For example, demonstrate with data how an AI platform can streamline content creation, enhance targeting, and ultimately boost ROI.

Engage Through Education: Organize interactive workshops or sessions where stakeholders can see the technology in action. This is about showing them how it resolves pain points, simplifies processes, and creates value.

For instance, setting up a live demonstration of an AI tool that predicts consumer behavior could reveal its potential to shape more effective campaigns, persuading stakeholders of its worth.

TECHNOLOGY EVALUATION

Once you have the green light from the top, it's time to dive deep into the tech world to pick what best suits your agency.

Comprehensive Research: Scrutinize each option for factors like scalability—will it grow with your business? Integration ease—how well does it mesh with your current tools? And, importantly, cost-effectiveness—is the investment justified by the benefits?

Real-world Application Example: When exploring AI for enhanced personalization, tools like Personyze offer an intriguing option. They adjust content in real-time based on user interaction, which could be a game-changer for client engagement and conversion rates.

IMPLEMENTATION PLANNING

With the right technology picked, a smooth rollout is next on the agenda.

Budgeting and Resource Allocation: Ensure you have the funds and support structures in place. This includes budgeting not only for the technology itself but also for any training and troubleshooting post-launch.

Training for Success: Prepare comprehensive training materials and sessions to familiarize your team with the new systems. The goal is to make the transition as smooth as possible, minimizing disruption and maximizing adoption.

For example, if you're introducing a sophisticated AI-driven analytics tool, plan a series of training sessions that cover everything from basic operations to advanced features, ensuring all team members are comfortable and competent with the technology.

Nurturing Skills: Continuous Training and Support

Tailored Training Programs: Implement training programs that ensure every team member is proficient and comfortable with the new technologies. Start with comprehensive sessions during the initial rollout and continue with ongoing support and refresher courses to keep skills sharp. For instance, if you're incorporating HubSpot's AI-powered Content Assistant, organize training sessions to help your team maximize its potential in content creation and optimization.

Ongoing Learning and Adaptation: It's not enough to train once and move on. Technology evolves, and so should your team's knowledge. Regularly scheduled training sessions, coupled with on-demand support, ensure that your team can tackle new challenges as they arise and make the most of the technology.

Evaluating Impact: Measure Success and Iterate

Feedback and Performance Metrics: Establish clear metrics to measure the effectiveness of the technology. Use both qualitative feedback from your team and quantitative data such as efficiency improvements, ROI, and customer satisfaction to gauge success. After integrating an AI-driven personalization tool, for example, closely monitor engagement rates and conversion metrics to understand its impact.

Cultivating Creativity

Encouraging Bold Ideas: Inspire an environment where taking calculated risks and innovating is the norm. Set up innovation labs or dedicated teams tasked with exploring new technologies. Encourage your team to experiment without fear of failure, as this is often where groundbreaking ideas are born.

Recognizing Contributions: Celebrate and reward creativity and successful integration of new technologies. Recognizing these efforts motivates the team and reinforces your agency's commitment to staying at the cutting edge.

The journey we've mapped out, spanning from training to nurturing a playground for innovation are the lifeblood practices that promise to revolutionize the heartbeat of your agency. By giving these dimensions top billing, you're buffing up your agency's muscles for today and armoring it for the battles of tomorrow.

The journey we've mapped out, spanning from training to nurturing a playground for innovation are the lifeblood practices that promise to revolutionize the heartbeat of your agency. By giving these dimensions top billing, you're buffing up your agency's muscles for today and armoring it for the battles of tomorrow.

GLOBAL GALLERY

AKQA's Commitment to Innovation: Leading Through Adaptability

As we look beyond our horizons, we see one agency in the global arena that has truly buffed up muscles of adaptability and prepared itself for future challenges, setting an example for us all—AKQA. Founded in 1994 by Ajaz Ahmed, a British entrepreneur who saw the immense potential of the internet and digital media, AKQA has grown to become a global digital design and communications powerhouse. Ahmed's early experiences with tech companies like Ashton-Tate, Ocean Software, and Apple UK fueled his passion for digital innovation and marketing, leading to the creation of AKQA.

AKQA's story is a vivid example of how staying adaptable and embracing innovation can carve out a leading spot in digital marketing. Let's explore the groundbreaking strategies and tech that have kept AKQA ahead of the curve.

Harnessing AI and Machine Learning

AKQA has brilliantly tapped into the power of AI and machine learning, revolutionizing their digital offerings. They've integrated these technologies into the core of their work, crafting deeply personalized, dynamic experiences that resonate with users. Take their partnership with Nike on the Nike Training Club app as a prime example. With AI, they've managed to offer workout recommendations that feel personally tailored, skyrocketing user engagement and satisfaction. But it's more than just tech wizardry; it's about genuinely understanding what users need and carefully shaping experiences that hit the mark every time.

Pioneering Use of Emerging Technologies

AKQA is always one step ahead, boldly embracing the future with their groundbreaking work in virtual reality (VR), augmented reality (AR), and blockchain. At the heart of their innovation is the Retail Centre of Excellence, a simulated in-store playground where they experiment with IoT, AI, and AR solutions.

Take, for example, the dazzling "Nike Unpack Your City" project. It's a showcase of how AR can skyrocket customer engagement. AKQA turned ordinary shoe boxes into interactive maps, creating a uniquely engaging experience. It's a perfect illustration of their knack for integrating creativity with technology in a way that feels effortlessly cool and utterly human.

Creativity and Collaboration

AKQA really stands out as a top-notch place to work for anyone who's into innovating, and that's got a lot to do with its awesome culture of creativity and working together. They've got this cool Story Lab and MVP Studio where people can throw around new ideas and whip up prototypes. It's all about multidisciplinary teams getting together in design sprints, creating a vibe where creativity just blooms.

Investment in Research and Development

AKQA really shows they're ahead of the game with their Accelerator Program. It's all about pushing the boundaries of innovation by using the latest research and tech to solve real-world issues. They make it a point to work closely with both industry leaders and academic circles, making sure they're always at the cutting edge of digital innovation.

Harnessing Data for Strategic Choices

Advanced analytics and insights are at the heart of what AKQA does. They use deep dives into data to really get what their clients need and to stay ahead of the game in a fast-changing market. Take their project with Delta Airlines, for example. By intelligently leveraging data analytics, AKQ created a customer experience that was both personalized and efficient.This approach led to happier and more loyal customers, showcasing the effectiveness of a data-driven strategy.

Ongoing Education and Evolution

AKQA actively embraces continuous learning and adaptation. They're all about keeping it fresh and informed, regularly hitting up industry conferences and pouring resources into training programs. This way, their team stays sharp and on top of the latest in digital marketing and tech advancements.

AKQA's passion for innovation and deep grasp of digital culture is truly inspiring. Their knack for constantly adapting and evolving is a testament to the incredible heights a digital marketing agency can reach with the right attitude and tools.

As you gaze into the future of your digital marketing agency, keep in mind that the digital tools we've talked about are your companions on a journey that's both long and shifting. Use these tools as you move forward, turning challenges into chances to shine.

CHAPTER 9

ZEN AND THE ART OF AGENCY MAINTENANCE

We are all digital wanderers, tackling the fast-paced, ever-changing digital maze every day. It's our bread and butter, and we've become experts at conquering this space. Yet, to sustain this success and keep winning in the digital world, we need something that contrasts sharply with the hustle culture we're so accustomed to: mindfulness and Zen.

As Chuang Tzu once observed, "To a mind that is still, the whole universe surrenders." This is the essence of Zen—finding calm in the chaos. It reminds us that as we take the first step in our journey, we need to draw from the peace and mindfulness around us to gather strength.

Why does this matter, especially towards the end of our journey, you might wonder? Here's the thing - in this wild world of clicks, codes, and campaigns, it turns out that peace is actually our secret superpower. By integrating mindfulness into our agency's culture, we can flip the script on pressure and turn it into productivity.

THE MINDFUL AGENCY

Let's dive into why mindfulness is super important for your digital marketing agency, especially for the leader steering the ship.

Mastering Decisions with Clarity

Mindfulness sharpens our decision-making skills, particularly in high-pressure scenarios where clarity is paramount. For example, when we were presented with a high-risk, high-reward project, instead of making a hasty decision, I chose to step back and reflect. This mindful approach allowed me to weigh the potential outcomes with a clear mind, leading to a well-thought-out contract that safeguarded our agency and secured a significant win. It's this kind of strategic thinking, fostered by mindfulness, that has continually propelled our agency forward.

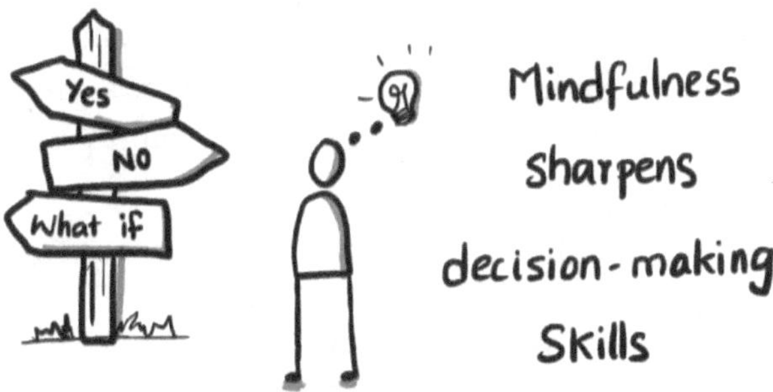

Strengthening Client Relationships Through Presence

Mindfulness also profoundly affects how we manage client relationships. Consider a critical moment when a valued client was considering parting ways due to unresolved issues. Rather than reacting hastily or defensively, I employed mindful listening. This approach allowed me to truly grasp their concerns and to address them in a manner that reaffirmed our commitment to their success. Not only did we manage to retain the client, but we also boosted their trust in us. This led to more referrals and opened up additional business opportunities.

Boosting Team Productivity with Mindful Leadership

Mindfulness goes beyond just finding personal peace; it's a potent way to boost the productivity of a team. When a leader maintains a calm and focused demeanor, it sets a positive tone for the entire team. During one of our most demanding campaigns, the stress levels were through the roof. I decided to introduce daily mindfulness sessions, giving everyone a chance to pause, breathe, and reset. These sessions weren't long—just 10 minutes each morning—but the impact was profound. The team became more focused and less stressed, leading to increased productivity and creativity. This ensured the campaign's success and impressed new clients who saw our efficiency and innovation firsthand. The boost in productivity translated into significant revenue and set a new standard for how we approached future projects.

Creating a Stable Workforce and Reducing Turnover

Employee turnover is a major concern for any business, but mindfulness can be a game-changer here. A workplace culture rooted in mindfulness promotes well-being and reduces burnout, leading to higher employee retention. By integrating mindfulness practices into our daily routine and emphasizing well-being, we created an environment where employees felt valued and supported. This shift led to a noticeable drop in turnover rates. With happier, more engaged employees, we reduced the costs associated with recruitment and training. This stability allowed us to build stronger, longer-lasting relationships with our clients, consistently delivering high-quality work. The result was a more cohesive team that enjoyed their work and contributed to the agency's overall success.

Securing Client Loyalty with Mindful Engagement

The power of mindfulness extends beyond internal team dynamics—it directly influences client satisfaction and loyalty. When clients interact with a team that's genuinely attentive and tuned into their needs, they feel valued and understood. This heightened level of service not only enhances client satisfaction but also fosters loyalty, making them more likely to stick with your agency long-term. For example, our regular client satisfaction surveys have consistently returned high praise for our team's mindful approach to service. This was clearly demonstrated when one of our longest-standing clients, deeply impressed by our consistent attentiveness and proactive service, referred us to three major new accounts. These referrals were not just a nod to our quality of service; they significantly boosted our revenue, accounting for a 20per cent increase within just six months. This example underscores how a mindful approach can lead to substantial business growth through enhanced client retention and referrals.

This strategic focus on mindfulness creates an outer environment where creativity, stability, and productivity flourish, making it an indispensable part of our agency's success formula.

THE BALANCED LEADER

We've talked a lot about the benefits of mindfulness for your digital marketing agency's success and growth. I know it might seem daunting to actually implement mindfulness in the hustle and bustle of an agency environment. I am often asked how can one genuinely incorporate mindfulness to refine decision-making and spur creativity.

That's why it's essential to start simple and start with you—the founders and leaders. In my role as an agency coach and someone who's launched and nurtured three agencies, I've lived through the high-speed, often chaotic life of digital marketing. This industry doesn't pause; it relentlessly pushes you towards quick decisions and rapid execution, which can lead to burnout and creativity blockages if not managed well. So, over the years, I've made it a point to integrate mindfulness techniques into my daily routine. Believe me, it's done wonders not just for my decision-making skills but also for sparking creativity and innovation in my teams. I'm keen to share some of the top practices that have really made a difference in how I lead and in my agency's performance.

The First Hour: Crafting a Calm and Strategic Start

Starting the day with a clear and calm mind has completely changed how productive I am and the overall vibe at our agency. It's all about creating a mood of mindfulness and purpose that spreads everywhere in the agency.

Here's how a typical morning unfolds for me:I get to the office by 9 AM with my ridiculously large coffee mug—the one my team teases could double as a plant pot. It sets the tone for the day. The office is wonderfully silent at this hour. With each sip, I take a moment to center myself, breathing in the calm and exhaling the rush. Then, I review the tasks for the day. I'm figuring out what needs to be tackled right away and what goals are key for the day as I strategize. This intentional approach gets me ready for the day and fills me and the whole team with a sense of purpose and direction. When the team steps in, they find a leader who is composed and thoroughly prepared, setting a positive example right from the start.

The 5-Minute Breather Break: A Quick Reset

Amid the relentless pace of the digital marketing world, the art of the pause has become a crucial tool in my daily arsenal. It's about granting yourself the permission to step back, if only for five minutes, to breathe and reboot. This practice has transformed how I handle the pressure and pace of my day.

Here's what this looks like in practice: Picture a day lined with back-to-back meetings, each one demanding a different facet of your strategic thinking and problem-solving skills.

Right after a particularly challenging client discussion—where the stakes were high and the tension palpable—I realized the need to clear my head. I stepped out for a quick five-minute break. Alone with my thoughts and a steaming cup of coffee in the fresh air, I allowed myself this moment to simply breathe and disconnect.

This small window to recharge did wonders. I returned with a warmer coffee and a cooler head. Refreshed and refocused, I was ready to dive into the next meeting with clarity and renewed vigor. These mini-breaks have become a staple in my routine, significantly boosting my productivity and well-being.

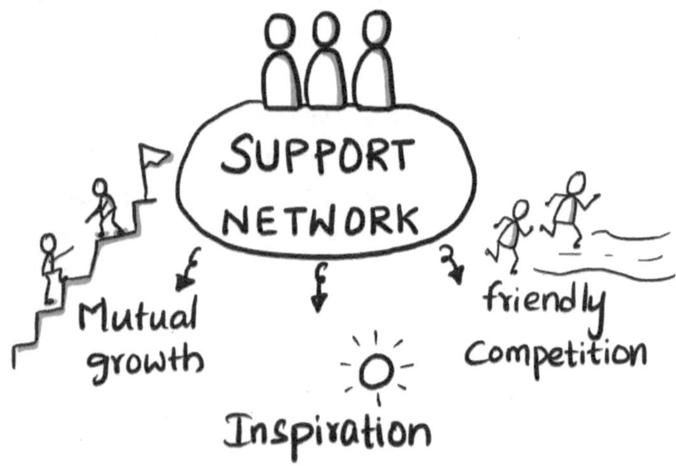

EXERCISE AND JOURNALING: THE UNDERSTATED MINDFULNESS PRACTICES

When we talk about mindfulness, we often think of meditation or deep breathing exercises, but two of the most potent practices are surprisingly simple: regular exercise and journaling. These activities pull us away from our screens and sharpen our mental clarity and creative thinking.

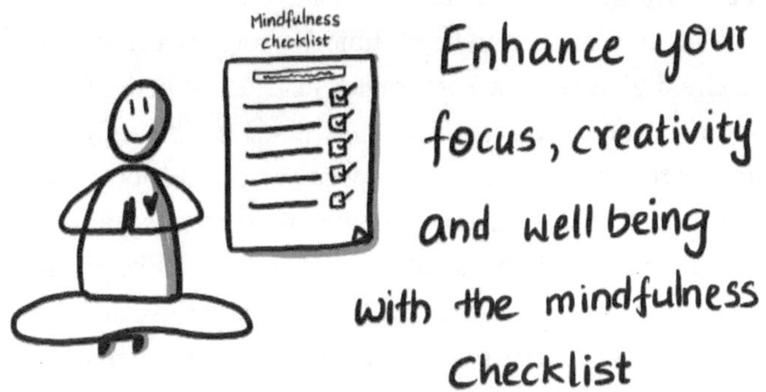

Exercise: The Physical Foundation for Mental Agility

Consistent physical activity has been a cornerstone of maintaining both my physical and mental health. Whether it's a brisk morning run, a yoga session to stretch and center myself, or a gym workout to really get the blood flowing, each form of exercise plays a vital role in keeping me energized and focused throughout the day.

I plan to squeeze in a 30-minute walk either at the beginning or end of my day. Walking through the nearby park, breathing in the fresh air, and moving my body is an invaluable reset button that clears my mind and sets a positive tone for whatever comes next. When I began incorporating a more structured exercise regimen into my routine, I noticed substantial improvements in my ability to handle stress and stay focused. On days I skip this routine, the difference in my productivity and mental sharpness is palpable.

Journaling: A Digital Detox for Creative Refresh

Away from the physicality of exercise, journaling offers a different kind of break—a mental one. Spending time each day to jot down thoughts, reflect on challenges, or even escape into a book on an entirely unrelated subject, provides a crucial pause from the digital chatter. Each night, just before bed, I dedicate about 15 minutes to read. This is where I deliberately choose topics far removed from my day-to-day work. This practice aids in winding down from the day and often sparks unexpected ideas that are incredibly valuable in my work. It's like giving my brain permission to wander in a field it doesn't usually play in, and the results often surprise me with new insights and renewed creativity.

As we continue exploring mindfulness, remember that these simple acts can forge a path to a more balanced, creative, and fulfilling professional life.

Talking out loud to yourself encourages openness + clarity

Talking Out Loud to Myself: A Pathway to Clarity

Adding to the value of mindfulness through exercise and journaling, I've discovered another incredibly helpful technique: talking out loud to myself. This might sound a bit unconventional, but it's incredibly effective for breaking down complex problems into manageable parts.

When our agency faced a significant drop in client engagements, the stress was palpable. I spent an afternoon in my office, talking through the problem out loud. This wasn't simply a stream of consciousness—it was a structured breakdown of what was going wrong and why. By vocalizing the challenges, I could map out the interconnected issues and their implications.

This method allowed me to identify critical areas that needed immediate attention and devise a clear, step-by-step action plan. But the benefits extended beyond just solving the problem at hand. Talking out loud helped me dissipate the stress cloud hanging over me. It transformed my approach from reactive to proactive leadership.

The impact was immediate and profound. I managed to chart a course out of the downturn, and this method instilled a greater sense of calm and purpose across the entire team. They were now part of a well-thought-out strategy that they could understand and support. This shift helped us tackle immediate issues and strengthened our resilience against future challenges.

Holistic health initiatives recharge creativity & health

That's why I stress that talking things out isn't just about solving problems; it's about demonstrating a mindset that encourages openness and clarity—qualities crucial for any leader tackling the high-stakes world of digital marketing.

A SUPPORT NETWORK: COLLABORATION AND FRIENDLY COMPETITION

Next, I want to emphasize how crucial it is to have a strong support network. It's not just about having people to turn to when times get tough; it's about creating a lively community that nurtures creativity, welcomes challenges, and provides steadfast support. This kind of network has been absolutely essential, providing immense value for personal development and a key strategic resource for the agency.

I recall connecting with a peer from a competing agency at a recent industry conference. Rather than maintaining a guarded distance, we saw an opportunity to collaborate. We exchanged perspectives on project management and client engagement, which sparked an idea for a joint initiative. We pooled our resources and expertise to tackle a project neither of us could have managed alone. The result was a successful campaign and a strengthened bond that led to mutual referrals. This approach has turned potential competitors into allies and has dramatically expanded our network and reach.

This shows the value of having a network of like-minded professionals. It creates a support system where sharing experiences and learning from each other becomes possible. It reduces the feeling of isolation that can come with leadership and offers fresh perspectives that can spark new ideas. Friendly competition keeps everyone on their toes, driving each other to achieve more.

These are transformative practices that touch every aspect of agency life.

Starting your day with that quiet first hour sets a calm, strategic tone, allowing you to plan with clarity and purpose. It's like laying out a map before a journey, ensuring you know exactly where you need to go and the stops you'll make along the way. Then, those 5-minute breather breaks throughout the day act as mini-oases, refreshing your mind and keeping your energy levels balanced amidst the chaos of back-to-back meetings.

The subtle power of regular exercise and the reflective practice of journaling cannot be overstated. They fortify your mental health and boost your creative energy, equipping you to tackle challenges with a sharper mind and a resilient spirit. Meanwhile, building a strong support network of peers ensures you're never alone in your journey. It's about creating a community that thrives on mutual growth, inspiration, and friendly competition.

YOUR MINDFULNESS ACTION CHECKLIST

After exploring how mindfulness can transform our professional and personal lives, let's put these insights into practice. If you're ready to make mindfulness a cornerstone of your leadership style, here's a practical checklist to guide you. This checklist will help ensure that your days are productive and balanced, making sure you're as grounded as the strategies you employ.

Time Management is King

Managing your time effectively is crucial. Use tools like Trello or Asana to keep things organized. Break your day into chunks—mornings for strategy, afternoons for client meetings, and evenings for creative work. Establish a daily 'No Meetings' hour to maintain focus and productivity.

Delegate Like a Pro

You can't do everything alone. Build a strong team and trust them. Empower your team to make decisions. For instance, my team managed a campaign for a major client while I was on vacation, and it was a success because they had the autonomy to act. Letting go can be challenging but is necessary for growth.

Self-Care Isn't Selfish

Self-care is vital for maintaining balance. Find what recharges you. Whether it's a walk in the park, reading a good book, daily meditation, or cooking, make it a non-negotiable part of your routine.

Embrace the Chaos, But Control It

The digital marketing world is unpredictable. Instead of resisting, build flexible plans. Always have a 'Plan B' for every major project. This way, when something unexpected happens, you're prepared.

Continuous Learning

Dedicate time each week to learn something new. This could be a webinar, podcast, or online course. For example, I once took a course on SEO trends that revamped our strategy and doubled our organic traffic within months.

Client Boundaries are Crucial

Set clear expectations with clients about your availability. Establish boundaries like no communication after 7 PM unless it's an emergency. This ensures you maintain a healthy work-life balance.

Celebrate Small Wins

Acknowledge and celebrate small victories. Whether it's closing a new client deal or delivering an outstanding campaign, these moments boost morale and reduce stress.

Tech Detox

Unplugging occasionally is essential. Have a 'Tech-Free' evening once a week. No laptops, no phones—just you and what makes you happy. For me, it's a weekly board game night with my family.

This checklist is a roadmap to a more mindful, balanced, and ultimately more successful leadership style. Each step is designed to enhance your focus, creativity, and wellbeing, ensuring you lead by example in every aspect of your digital marketing journey.

Wellness Strategies for a Thriving Agency

So far, we've explored how to cultivate mindfulness within yourself as a leader and witnessed its positive effects rippling through your agency. Now, let's focus on embedding mindfulness and wellness into the very core of your agency, ensuring that everyone thrives together.

Introducing wellness and mindfulness into our business model has done wonders for productivity and has nurtiled a healthier, more creative workplace vibe. Here's a peek at some of the strategies we've rolled out and the effects they've had on our team and the business's bottom line.

Flexible Breaks: Encouraging Regular Resets

One standout strategy that's reshaping our work environment is the implementation of flexible breaks. This approach allows team members to take breaks as needed, recognizing that brief pauses can significantly recharge one's mental batteries and enhance productivity.

At our agency, we see breaks not as time off, but as essential intervals that enable our team to maintain their creative output over long periods. This policy caters to individual needs—whether it's stepping out for a breath of fresh air, meditating for a few minutes, or simply grabbing a coffee. It's about understanding that mental rest is not synonymous with idleness; rather, it's a vital component of sustained intellectual labor.

For example, consider the experience of one of our graphic designers, who was hitting a creative wall on a high-profile project. The pressure was mounting, and traditional brainstorming methods were leading nowhere. Recognizing her frustration, we encouraged her to step away from her desk and take a walk outside. Just 15 minutes later, she returned with a refreshed perspective and sparked an idea that broke the deadlock and exceeded our client's expectations. This minor pause in her day made a significant impact, underscoring the value of our flexible break policy.

This approach helps prevent burnout, keeps our team engaged, and promotes a healthier, more productive work environment that naturally inspires innovation and success.

ASSESSING AND ADDRESSING INCOMPETENCE VS. CREATIVE FATIGUE

In the fast-paced world of digital marketing, it's easy to misinterpret a dip in productivity. It's essential to distinguish whether the root cause is incompetence or creative fatigue. Creative fatigue occurs when continuous mental effort leads to a decline in performance. It's not a lack of skill but a sign that the brain needs rest and rejuvenation.

Regular performance reviews are our primary tool for making this distinction. These reviews are about understanding the underlying reasons for performance issues. By creating an open and supportive environment, we encourage our team to communicate their struggles openly, which allows us to provide the right kind of support.

For instance, during a performance review, we noticed one of our copywriters, who was usually on top of her game, was consistently missing deadlines. Instead of jumping to conclusions, we delved deeper to understand the issue. It turned out that she was experiencing creative fatigue, not a decline in competence. She felt overwhelmed and uninspired after handling several demanding projects back-to-back without adequate breaks.

Recognizing this, we encouraged her to take more frequent breaks and provided additional resources to help reignite her creativity. We also adjusted her workload temporarily to give her the space she needed to recover. The result was remarkable. She regained her productivity and confidence, delivering some of her best work shortly after.

By addressing the root cause of performance issues and distinguishing between incompetence and creative fatigue, we ensure that our team remains engaged, motivated, and productive. This approach creates a supportive work environment where employees feel valued and understood, ultimately driving the agency's success.

WELLNESS PROGRAMS: RECHARGING CREATIVITY AND HEALTH

We've infused our agency's culture with wellness programs that go beyond the typical perks. These programs are carefully tailored to nurture both the physical and mental well-being of our team. Let's explore how integrating holistic health initiatives like yoga, meditation, and fitness classes has transformed our workplace dynamics.

Holistic Health Initiatives Spark Productivity and Inspiration

Our commitment to wellness has introduced yoga sessions, on-site meditation breaks, and even group fitness challenges. These are not just activities; they are our way of saying that health is a priority. We've noticed that these moments of pause significantly elevate energy levels and focus. For example, by enabling flexible breaks, we've seen a decrease in burnout rates. Employees return from these pauses refreshed and ready to tackle complex projects with renewed vigor.

A standout story is from a team member who took advantage of our "work from anywhere" policy. Choosing to work from a serene beach in Goa, they found the change of scenery refreshing and inspiring. This freedom resulted in a surge of creativity and productivity that led to one of our most successful campaigns of the year. The campaign boosted our client's brand and set a new benchmark for creativity in our team.

Fostering Creativity Through Well-being

It's fascinating to observe how wellness initiatives contribute directly to enhancing creativity. Incorporating mental health support and encouraging digital detoxes have allowed our team members to unplug and reconnect with their creative sides. For instance, after a digital detox challenge, our creative team gathered to brainstorm, free from digital distractions. The result was nothing short of phenomenal—a campaign inspired by traditional Indian art that won an industry award and earned praise from our clients for its authenticity.

Strengthening Bonds Through Shared Wellness Experiences

Another transformative aspect of our wellness programs has been their impact on team morale and cohesion. Initiatives like group fitness challenges and joint outdoor adventures have been particularly effective. These activities build deeper connections among team members. For instance, our unforgettable trek in the Himalayas was a crucible for forging stronger bonds. Team members supported each other through physical challenges and shared awe-inspiring moments, creating lasting bonds. This sense of camaraderie has made collaboration smoother and more intuitive back at the office, leading to more efficient project execution.

Direct Impact on Business Outcomes

The positive atmosphere nurtured by our wellness initiatives extends beyond morale; it translates directly into stellar business performance. When our team is healthy, happy, and united, their productivity soars, and creativity flows freely. This led to a tangible improvement in ou``r agency's bottom line.Since rolling out our wellness strategies, we've maintained a 90per cent client retention rate and seen a remarkable 120per cent increase in revenue over the past year.

These wellness strategies show that taking care of your team's health does more than just boost personal well-being. It actually leads to real business success, making us more innovative and helping us deliver top-notch results.

GLOBAL GALLERY

Exploring SocialB's Journey to Mindfulness and Well-being

Let's take a look around the world and zoom in on SocialB, a digital marketing agency that's making waves with its sharp strategic skills and heartfelt dedication to integrating mindfulness throughout its corporate culture. SocialB's method shines a light on how to create a resilient and flourishing workplace by deeply integrating well-being practices.

SocialB's well-being team stands at the core of their efforts, dedicated entirely to nurturing a supportive work environment. They focus on the human element. By organizing simple yet impactful activities like casual coffee catch-ups and engaging weekly challenges, they ensure everyone at SocialB feels included and valued. It's initiatives like these that transform an ordinary workplace into a thriving community.

Mindfulness and Physical Wellness

At SocialB, they recognize that the well-being of their team is paramount, integrating regular yoga and mindfulness sessions into the workday. These are a vital part of the day that helps everyone reset and refocus. The feedback speaks volumes—employees report greater clarity and reduced stress, proving how essential these moments of calm are in a high-energy field.

Emphasizing Mental Health

Mental health is not a side note at SocialB; it's a priority. The agency has cultivated an environment where talking about mental health is encouraged, ensuring that no one has to mask their struggles. Resources and support are always available, making it clear that the company values mental well-being just as much as professional achievement.

Wellness Adapted for Remote Work

When the pandemic hit, SocialB didn't miss a beat; they adapted their supportive practices for a remote setting seamlessly. Regular virtual sessions and open lines of communication ensured that working from home didn't mean working in isolation. Their proactive approach t enhanced the team's health and productivity during uncertain times.

Interactive Well-being Initiatives

SocialB keeps wellness engaging and interactive with creative challenges like Wellbeing Bingo. These involve fostering a sense of camaraderie and ongoing engagement in healthful practices.

At SocialB, integrating well-being into the company ethos has revolutionized not just how employees feel but also how they perform. Here's a closer look at the transformative effects of their wellness initiatives:

Job Satisfaction Soars

SocialB's dedication to the mental and physical health of its team members has fostered a sense of genuine care and support within the workplace.As a result, people stick around. They're happier, more engaged, and deeply connected to the agency's mission, reducing turnover and building a stable, committed team.

Productivity on the Rise

When wellness is prioritized, productivity naturally follows. At SocialB, employees who feel good, mentally and physically, bring their 'A' game every day. This entails empowering them to perform at their best, unhindered by stress or burnout.

Client Relationships Strengthen

Happy employees lead to happy clients. At SocialB, the positive effects of the agency's wellness culture extend beyond internal metrics to touch every client interaction. Employees who are engaged and satisfied are more creative and proactive, qualities that shine through in their work and bolster client satisfaction and loyalty.

Ensuring a Vibrant Business Future

SocialB's holistic approach to well-being sets the stage for long-term success. A team that's healthy and motivated is a team that's ready to face whatever challenges come their way, ensuring the agency remains dynamic and competitive in the ever-evolving digital marketing field.

SocialB's strategy showcases the profound impact of integrating wellness deeply into business practices. It's a clear win for everyone involved: employees thrive, productivity soars, and clients reap the benefits of innovative and spirited service.

Remember, what we have talked about here in the context of mindfulness involves adopting a mindset that values balance and clarity, especially in the crazy world of digital marketing. Every intentional move you make keeps your agency in the mix and helps shape the digital world.

Let's look ahead, equipped with what we need to create a work environment where creativity flourishes in a peaceful atmosphere. This is about building a place where we tackle each challenge with a clear head and grab every chance with keen focus.

ONWARD: THE PATH AHEAD

As you step away from these pages, think of this journey as the beginning, not the end. Starting a digital agency is one thing, but building one that can grow, evolve, and thrive? That's where the real magic happens. The insights, strategies, and lessons shared here serve as the building blocks for creating something meaningful—something that resonates with your unique vision and values.

The road ahead won't always be easy, and there will be times that really challenge your determination. But it's during these tough moments that real growth takes place. When you look back, you'll realize that the heart of your success isn't just about what you create but also about how you approach things and the mindset you cultivate. As an entrepreneur, your mindset is what drives everything forward. It's what gets you through the tough days, what fuels your passion, and what enables you to see opportunities where others see obstacles. Without the right mindset, even the best-laid plans can falter.

My own journey has taught me that resilience is key. You need to be able to adapt, to pivot when necessary, and to keep going when things don't go as planned. The marketing industry is always evolving, sometimes at a dizzying pace, and staying relevant requires that same agility. It's about being proactive, staying curious, and continuously learning. But resilience isn't just about bouncing back from challenges; it's about embracing them as opportunities for growth.

One mantra I've held onto throughout my entrepreneurial journey is to "aim for redundancy." That might sound counterintuitive, but hear me out. As a leader, your goal should be to build a business that can run smoothly without you being involved in every little detail. It's about creating a structure that's so well-designed that you've made yourself unnecessary in the day-to-day operations. This doesn't mean you step away from leadership; it means you've empowered your team and put the right processes in place so the business can thrive independently.

Let me leave you with one final story to bring home the significance of this mantra. When I first started working, it wasn't in the world of digital marketing but as an intern at my father's newspaper. Our Editor-in-Chief, Mr. Vijay Phanshikar, who has been at the helm for over 40 years was my mentor during that time. Each week, he would hand me a book to read, and my assignment was to summarize it and present my analysis to him—on top of all my other duties. One day, out of the blue, he handed me a crumpled piece of paper with a question scribbled on it: "What is the most important task for a leader?"

I spent days coming up with answers. I listed every creative idea I could think of—vision, strategy, decision-making—but every single time, Mr. Phanshikar would look at me and simply say, "No." This went on for weeks, and eventually, I gave up. That's when he came over to my desk and left another crumpled piece of paper. It had just one line: "The most important task for a leader is to aim to become redundant."

That was the moment it all clicked. True leadership is about building something that can thrive without you. It's about putting systems in place, empowering your team, and ensuring that the business runs as smoothly in your absence as it does with your presence. That's the ultimate test of leadership—and it's a mindset that has stuck with me ever since.

This book, in many ways, is your sneak peek into establishing and growing your service business with this mindset at its core. It's about cultivating an environment where you, as a leader, empower your team to such an extent that you can step back and watch the machine run smoothly, knowing it can operate without your constant oversight.

I've built my businesses on this mantra through years of trial and error, victories, and missteps, and now I'm passing these hard-earned lessons on to you. What you choose to do with them will shape the next phase of your journey. It's your path to carve, your story to write.

But remember, success doesn't happen overnight, and it's not a race to the finish line. It's about perseverance, adaptability, and the steady pursuit of growth. Your progress may be slow at times, but as long as you keep learning and evolving, you'll get there.

As Steve Jobs famously said, "The people who are crazy enough to think they can change the world are the ones who do." So go out there, take that bold step, build your agency with intention, and create something that stands the test of time.

ABOUT THE AUTHOR

ARCHANA PUROHIT

BUSINESS COACH, ENTREPRENEUR, AND ANGEL INVESTOR

Archana Purohit is a seasoned entrepreneur, digital marketing expert, and Angel Investor with over 17 years of experience in building and scaling businesses. As a fourth-generation entrepreneur, Archana has seamlessly combined traditional business values with forward-thinking digital strategies to become a trusted leader in the industry.

Her journey started as the youngest Mumbai Bureau Head at *Franchise India Media*, followed by her instrumental role in driving the digital transformation of *The Hitavada*, Central India's largest English daily. In 2018, she founded *Digital Ozone* with modest capital and transformed it into a leading digital marketing agency, serving over 100 brands across FinTech, EdTech, and HealthTech sectors. Even during challenging times like the pandemic, Archana's strategic leadership ensured a 90per cent client retention rate.

Her success led to the acquisition of *Digital Ozone* by eYantra Industries, where she became CEO, leading a ₹500 crore turnover business with a team of 70+ professionals. Archana's sharp business acumen and ability to scale ventures have earned her recognition in Business World's 40 Under 40 list.

Over the past year, Archana has expanded her focus to mentoring and coaching digital marketing startup founders, helping them scale effectively. As a mentor at *T-Hub*, she guides startups through their go-to-market strategies and growth plans, using her deep experience to shape their success. She is also working on her latest venture, *Agency Adda*, a marketplace designed to connect marketing agencies with businesses, creating a vibrant ecosystem for agencies to grow and collaborate.

An alumna of the Indian School of Business (ISB), Archana is passionate about empowering the next generation of entrepreneurs. Her upcoming book will share actionable insights on building and scaling digital marketing businesses, offering valuable guidance for anyone looking to succeed in today's competitive digital landscape.

Archana's proven expertise, combined with her commitment to fostering entrepreneurial growth, positions her as a key voice in the digital marketing world. Her book is set to become an essential guide for aspiring entrepreneurs and marketers seeking to make their mark.

www.ingramcontent.com/pod-product-compliance
Lightning Source LLC
LaVergne TN
LVHW091315150826
845673LV00006B/1650

* 9 7 9 8 8 9 6 3 2 3 6 2 4 *